"Dannah Gresh has hit on a simple yet undiscovered truth that puts seemingly random questions of sexuality in context. I love the way Dannah doesn't shy away from or water down the tough issues, yet she *never* compromises God's best for you! This is a must-read for any single Christian woman."

  —DR. JULI SLATTERY, clinical psychologist, Focus on the Family,
   and author of *No More Headaches*

"Dannah Gresh has totally nailed it with this pertinent and hugely needed book. Written honestly and compellingly, this is a must-read for all teenage girls—wait, this is a must-read for everyone, especially teenage guys! I am so grateful for this important resource and plan to recommend it to all my young adult readers."

  —MELODY CARLSON, author of Diary of a Teenage Girl series
   and the TrueColor series

"Dannah Gresh hits another home run! *What Are You Waiting For?* is refreshingly real and relevant—definitely a timely message for today's generation of young women!"

  —SHANNON ETHRIDGE, international speaker and best-selling
   author of *Every Young Woman's Battle*

"This is hands-down the best book about sexual fidelity I have ever read—informative, entertaining, and *very* inspiring. Dannah Gresh tackles the trickiest of topics with astonishing grace. Her explanation of the sacred power of sex is unblushing and revelatory. I know this is a book for girls, but every Christian guy should read it too. I'm already reading it for the second time."

  —NATE LARKIN, founder of the Samson Society and author
   of *Samson and the Pirate Monks: Calling Men to Authentic
   Brotherhood*

"If you are looking for the gospel truth on the very real issue of sex and sexuality that all singles face, this is the book for you. Dannah Gresh talks to singles where they really live. Not only is it refreshing, it is liberating—

as truth always is. Dannah does not dance around the issues but addresses them with in-your-face clarity that is sorely needed. Sharing the spiritual implications while balancing the reality of the natural world we live in, Dannah practically addresses how singles can be victorious in the battle between the flesh and the spirit."

—MICHELLE MCKINNEY HAMMOND, author of *What Women Don't Know and Men Don't Tell You*

"All I can say is *wow!* My assistant's teenage daughter agreed to flip through this book for me as a favor and ended up absorbed in the entire thing! As she rightly put it, *What Are You Waiting For?* brings 'amazing insight into what no one tells you about sex—and it really can strengthen the relationship you have with God and your future spouse.' This book is a fantastic read. Dannah Gresh has such a special way of taking an important subject and making it appealing, practical, and accessible to everyone."

—SHAUNTI FELDHAHN, best-selling author of *For Women Only* and *For Young Women Only*

"In an age where sex is perverted and belittled—when it appears to be a tool in the hands of the Enemy rather than the God who created it—Dannah has shown us God's pure intention for sexuality. Through an in-depth study of Scripture and confirmation in life experiences, she highlights the honest-to-goodness biblical truth behind one of life's most precious and beautiful mysteries. Women young and old will read this book and find the inspiration and tools they need to treat God's gift of sexuality with the respect and protection it deserves."

—JULIE HIRAMINE, founder of Generations of Virtue and author of *Beautifully Made*

"*What Are You Waiting For?* is a well-written study of the sexual culture our teens are immersed in today and offers a culturally relevant perspective that aligns itself with the Word of God. Dannah has managed to walk the fine line of approaching this difficult subject in a way that will inspire teens to live holy lives and inspire parents to broach this delicate topic with their kids. This book is not for the faint of heart; however, neither is raising teenagers in our current society."

—RON LUCE, founder and president of Teen Mania Ministries

what are you
waiting for?

what are you waiting for?

The One Thing No One Ever Tells You About Sex

Dannah Gresh

WATERBROOK
PRESS

WHAT ARE YOU WAITING FOR?
PUBLISHED BY WATERBROOK PRESS
12265 Oracle Boulevard, Suite 200
Colorado Springs, Colorado 80921

All Scripture quotations, unless otherwise indicated, are taken from the Holy Bible, New International Version®. NIV®. Copyright © 1973, 1978, 1984 by Biblica Inc.™ Used by permission of Zondervan. All rights reserved worldwide. www.zondervan.com. Scripture quotations marked (NKJV) are taken from the New King James Version®. Copyright © 1982 by Thomas Nelson Inc. Used by permission. All rights reserved. Scripture quotations marked (NASB) are taken from the New American Standard Bible®. © Copyright The Lockman Foundation 1960, 1962, 1963, 1968, 1971, 1972, 1973, 1975, 1977, 1995. Used by permission. (www.Lockman.org). Scripture quotations marked (ESV) are taken from The Holy Bible, English Standard Version, copyright © 2001 by Crossway Bibles, a division of Good News Publishers. Used by permission. All rights reserved. Scripture quotations marked (KJV) are taken from the King James Version.

Italics in Scripture quotations reflect the author's added emphasis.

Details in some anecdotes and stories have been changed to protect the identities of the persons involved.

ISBN 978-1-60142-331-3
ISBN 978-1-60142-332-0 (electronic)

Cover design by Leslie E. Seetin

Published in the United States by WaterBrook Multnomah, an imprint of the Crown Publishing Group, a division of Random House Inc., New York.

WATERBROOK and its deer colophon are registered trademarks of Random House Inc.

Library of Congress Cataloging-in-Publication Data
Gresh, Dannah.
      What are you waiting for? : the one thing no one ever tells you about sex / Dannah Gresh.
— 1st ed.
            p. cm.
      Includes bibliographical references.
      ISBN 978-1-60142-331-3 — ISBN 978-1-60142-332-0 (electronic)
   1. Chastity. 2. Teenage girls—Religious life. 3. Young women—Religious life. 4. Sexual abstinence—Religious aspects—Christianity. 5. Sex instruction for youth—Religious aspects—Christianity. I. Title.
      BV4647.C5G74 2011
      241'.66—dc22

                                                        2010034596

Printed in the United States of America
2011—First Edition

10 9 8 7 6 5 4 3 2 1

SPECIAL SALES
Most WaterBrook Multnomah books are available at special quantity discounts when purchased in bulk by corporations, organizations, and special-interest groups. Custom imprinting or excerpting can also be done to fit special needs. For information, please e-mail SpecialMarkets@WaterBrookMultnomah.com or call 1-800-603-7051.

To Bob

who is writing a *yada* love story with me
so the world can see the mysterious love story
of Christ and the church.

contents

let's get real

this book is not for spiritual monks.

If you spend more of your time at church getting to know God's Word than out in the world living it, you probably won't like this book. It's raw and real. If you can't handle words like *masturbation, orgasm,* and *porn,* you should just put it down now. These are real-world words that real people use.

Frankly, I wish I didn't have to use them. I find a more poetic, subtle approach to sexuality more romantic. Not to mention tasteful. It seems to me that the Bible—while not lacking in sexual instruction, ethic, and purpose—often presents the subject in veiled terms, leaving us unblushed by its modest references to a gift so tender. I'd like to write more like that, and I have in previous books, but not this one.

We don't live in a modest world. And the fact is, I'm not a spiritual monk.

And you probably aren't either.

My intention isn't to shock you as I approach this topic more directly than I have before. And I don't think I will. It's not as if you haven't heard about oral sex or girls kissing girls. My intention is to be relevant and to bring some practical clarity to the sadly common temptations our culture presses at you. I believe this is also a biblical approach. After all, think about the two letters Paul sent to the Corinthian church. While many subjects are covered in these letters and we can't be sure exactly what was in the letters *from* the church to the apostle that precipitated his response, it seems that the Corinthians were asking a lot of practical questions about marriage and sex. They were conflicted by the promiscuous culture that surrounded them. So they wondered, "Is it even good to be married?" (Perhaps you wonder that too.) "Because sex is perverted, shouldn't we also abstain in marriage?" (That one was way off course!) "If my spouse is unsaved, should I get divorced?"

The apostle answered their questions.

One by one.

He clearly addressed their uncertainties and confusion—and I hope to do the same for you. Well, I hope we can find some answers together. If you press into your questions and I press into my research, we can link the two to find some answers to the questions our cultural experiences tend to raise.

You and I live in a rather promiscuous culture, and questions about sex burn through our minds. And while I really hope you'll build a great sexual theology as you think over what you find in these pages, I also want you to have a practical understanding of how to live it out. So I've spent a lot of time with college-aged young women in intimate conversation about the burning questions that run through their heads—the ones the world tries to address in its sexual excess but the church often runs from.

"Is masturbation a sin?"

"How do I know if he's the one?"

"What if he has a problem with porn?"

"What if I'm a lesbian?"

And hold on to your seat—there's more!

It is my hope that these very direct, very practical pages will give you the answers you need to live out what you believe. After all, what good is a sexual theology if it doesn't speak to the issues of this contemporary day and age, where few are spiritual monks?

So what am I if not a spiritual monk?

Am I a girl gone wild?

No.

I am a biblical woman who loves God's Word and feasts on it each day.

I am a sinful woman who has been healed by the perfecting love of my Savior.

I am a wife and mother who is honored to serve the Father in those roles.

I am an author empowered by the Holy Spirit to write and live out Truth.

I am a girl who occasionally watches *The Ellen Show,* and I think she's sweet and funny and generous.

And that's where it starts to get complicated—when my private, God-loving self interacts with a real world that doesn't acknowledge Him as God. Just like you, I am trying to live out my faith in a very crazy world. Which is why I'm so glad to have found some tremendous clarity in God's Word, which gives you and me a very clear definition of sex to consider. This definition answers every burning question and is thoroughly relevant for today. Once I discovered it, confusion over sexual questions was easy to resolve. I even came to understand why as a little girl I was predisposed to dressing up like a princess and dreaming that my prince would one day come. No one taught me to do that. It was a natural yearning as my heart began its search for my life partner.

For me, that dream came to its culmination during a thrilling moment of made-for-TV romance!

I was in college, and I was in love. Had been for two years. One problem: my prince was graduating, while I was obligated to one more year of servitude at Cedarville University. My boyfriend, Bob, had a

engagement hazing

Pity the guy who falls in love on a Christian college campus, where the traditional hazing of a newly engaged couple is unique from the state school or private institution. If you get engaged on one of these campuses, here's what's in store, according to my friends on Facebook, whose experiences may vary a bit from that of other grads from these schools:

Cedarville University	the guy gets thrown into Cedar Lake
Grove City College	the guy gets "creeked" in Wolf Creek
Patrick Henry College	the guy gets "bobtized" on Lake Bob

part in "Senior Night," a hilariously dramatic look back at the class's four years. Naturally I planned to attend, but my heart was so sad. In fewer than twenty-four hours, he would be gone and I would be left behind for a quiet summer of classes.

After a quick bite at Colonial Pizza, Bob and I made our way to the university's chapel. I found some friends to sit with. He made his way backstage.

I laughed my way through much of the night, but then Dr. Jim Phipps and Professor Meg Wheeler, the night's emcees, began to talk about all the guys who'd recently been thrown into Cedar Lake. Getting thrown into the lake was every guy's reward for flashing a diamond

Moody Bible Institute	the guy gets duct-taped to the flagpole
Wheaton College	both get to climb Blanchard Tower and ring the bell
Wesleyan College	the girl gets thrown into the water fountain
Trinity International University	the girl gets "candle lighted"

Just in case you're in the dark about "candle lighting," let me illuminate you! All the girls on a dorm floor are called together by a Candle Lighter, who's been secretly notified of the engagement. The leader passes an unlit candle around, and when it gets to the newly engaged girl, she lights it while her dorm mates squeal in delighted celebration. Then they listen with rapt attention to her proposal story.

in front of his girl and hearing the word yes. A rite of passage coveted by every college couple, lake activity was rampant just before graduation. A yearning washed over me as they talked about all the happy proposals.

"What would a proposal like that look like?" The question was posed. And I wondered along with the audience.

Then...

Bob Gresh came out onto the stage...

...with a black velvet box in his hand.

He was searching for me in the audience as the spotlight followed him.

My heart was thumping so heavily that I was certain it was shaking the solid twenty-foot pew I sat on—and everyone sitting on it with me.

"And then I'd take her by the hand," he said, offering the audience the play-by-play as he approached me.

"And I'd lead her to the stage." I followed him as he talked.

A single chair was waiting for me. I plopped into it, weak at the knees.

Then my prince bowed on one knee and took my left hand in his. "Dannah Barker," he asked, looking lovingly into my eyes, "will you marry me?"

I paused.

Tears welling.

My breath had truly been taken by the moment. Apparently so had the breath of everyone in the audience, who had now caught on to the fact that this was real. And some lovesick twenty-one-year-old guy had just put his heart out for the taking or rejecting. The only sound in my ears was my loudly thumping heart and Bob's nervous breathing.

Finally I nodded and barely mouthed the answer: "Yes!"

Bob slipped a brilliant diamond onto my left ring finger and then stood, pumping his fist into the air in victory. The audience collectively took a deep breath and then jumped to their feet in wild applause.

My prince had come!

I recently reached the milestone of being with him more years than I've lived without him, and he has spent *all* of those years romancing me. It's never, ever stopped. Girl, this is the kind of guy you

Quirky Proposals

I've heard about some pretty quirky proposals. There was the guy who carved his proposal into sixteen pumpkins and one who posted it on twenty-three hay bales. But most astonishing of all was one where the quirk took an unexpected twist: Reed Harris decided to pop the question to Kaitlin Whipple by hiding a ring in her Wendy's Frosty. Unfortunately, Reed also invited Kaitlin's friends to witness the moment, and one of them challenged her to a Frosty-drinking race. The poor girl swallowed the ring whole. Reed had to drive her to the hospital so she could actually see it—on an x-ray![1]

want to marry. I'm talking about the kind of guy who welcomes you home from a long trip with lit candles leading the way to a bubble bath so you can relax. I'm talking about the kind of guy who whisks you away to New York City, having arranged for the two of you to spend days visiting every scene from your favorite romantic movie until your heart melts. I'm talking about the kind of guy who texts insane love notes to you all hours of the day. (Last month's goofiest text was, "I love you more than Toast Chees." Unless you understand how much the man loves Toast Chee crackers, you cannot appreciate the romance of that one!)

Do you want that kind of never-ending romance (okay, minus the Toast Chees)? Dare to dig in with me for a few raw and real chapters about God, sex, and romance. Let me start in the next chapter by backing up a few years from Bob's amazing marriage proposal to a time when I was asking a lot of questions myself.

clearly confused

it was during my lunch break.

I was walking across Beaver Avenue, sipping the remainder of my iced tea, when a question changed the course of my life.

A freshman in college, I was serving an internship at my parents' award-winning radio station for the summer. While I had loved my week of studying in the pressure cooker of a copywriting room, the current week's excruciating look at radio sales had me making promises to my introverted self that I would never—I repeat *never*—be in sales. (Two years later, I got my first job with a Penn State football magazine as—you guessed it—their salesgirl!) But, for the moment, I was dreaming of being a writer and *enduring* a week of selling.

The one bright hope of this week was the intriguing saleswoman: Greek Goddess, 3WZ's top-selling star, had been handpicked by my dad as the agent I would shadow. He trusted her to teach me well and be a great role model. With big brown eyes and perfectly white teeth that contrasted with her beautiful Greek skin, she was as polished as a twentysomething woman could be. Her shiny leather business heels perfectly complemented her equally shiny manicured nails and carefully ironed suit.

We'd just discussed cold-calling, over deli sandwiches, and were headed back to the station when Greek Goddess veered way off the course of professional dialogue and into something very personal.

What's in a Name?

I just loathe fictional stories in a nonfiction book. You won't find any in here. Just real live girls like you and me. Sometimes their stories are very revealing. When that's the case, I've changed their names to protect their privacy. I'd do the same for you! If I have particularly strong images of the person, I may take the liberty to make up a name—like Greek Goddess!

"Dannah, I know your parents are really conservative, but you *do* know it's perfectly acceptable to have sex with a guy when you are in love. You're in college. You can make your own decisions now. I know you've been with your guy a long time. It's natural to be sexually active, and it's perfectly okay. Just be smart about it. I'm here for you if you need to talk." She rambled on, her dazzling white teeth chattering away. Then she matter-of-factly asked a question that woke me up.

"Do you need me to get you some condoms?"

The question was a grenade, and I hadn't been trained to take cover. I slowed in my steps when it hit, forced to confront the internal war I'd been ignoring in my soul.

"Are you having sex with your boyfriend?" she asked.

"No, I am not having sex with my boyfriend," I asserted, perhaps too adamantly. I reasoned with myself: *I'm not having sex with him. Not now. Not at this moment. Not at any time in the...very...recent... past.*

"But you *have* had sex with him?" she said, stopping to look me in the eyes.

There it was. The only question other than "Do you need me to get you some condoms?" that could have stopped me *completely* in my tracks. It was the one that would change my life, forcing me to answer a myriad of related questions to either defend the honest answer or bring me to a place of repentance over it. I stood there, bloodied by my own battle, looking into Greek Goddess's eyes, and saw a moment of fifteen-year-old passion flash past, as if recorded to taunt me in replay. That moment of passion—and my conflict over it—had kept me with this guy that time would prove was not "the one."

"We aren't having sex," I said flatly. We weren't. And had agreed not to—but that didn't mean we hadn't. We were way past condoms. This was no longer a physical issue in my life, but the World War of My Soul. I had to decide if I believed what my mom and dad had taught me or what Greek Goddess advocated.

———

A sexual debate is taking place today that is critical to the future of our society—and it's been rattling on for quite a few years. One side says condoms and sexual freedom are the answer to youthful clamoring about sex. The other slides silver rings on the fingers of teens and hopes these miniature chastity belts will protect them in moments of temptation. Who's right? Who's wrong? Is there a middle ground? Can anybody claim to have clear and certain answers?

Yep.

I do.

That day on Beaver Avenue, I began searching for not only the answer to *why* I believed what I believed but also *how* to live it out successfully. And I found something that's going to blow you away.

I know it's a big claim, but so is a subtitle that reads "The One Thing No One Ever Tells You About Sex," don't you think? I don't claim this with pride. In truth, I can't believe I have the privilege of showing you this amazing, wonderful, mind-blowing truth. Hundreds and hundreds of people make a living by talking about sex (and countless more by joking about it or portraying it on-screen). Yet not once have I heard anyone talk about what I'm going to share with you in this book. Not once. Strangely, many step right on top of this secret treasure and don't even know it is underfoot.

Let me promise you this: there is one thing no one has told you about sex. Without this critical piece of truth, your personal sexual choices will remain muddled. But once you grasp this simple yet amazing concept, you will find clarity to answer all the questions swirling around sexuality, including, "What are you waiting for?"

Just a few years ago, I stumbled upon a carefully veiled but not deeply hidden labyrinth into God's mind concerning sex. (Hey, since God came up with the concept of sex, He should know a thing or two about how it works best, right?) I found His thoughts hidden in an ancient language, and I've never looked at things the same way again.

No one who hears this does. When I step off the stage after sharing it, people chase me down to declare, "That's it!"

Those two words sum up the revelatory power of what I'm about to share with you. "That's what?" you may be asking.

"That's it…the reason I'm so sex-crazed!"

"That's it…the reason it's so sacred!"

"That's it…the reason it hurt so much when I handled it casually!"

"That's it…the reason I've never found satisfaction in my dozens of sexual conquests!"

"That's it…the reason I am so intrigued!"

"That's it…the reason God created us to be sexual!"

Everyone has his or her own personal "That's it!" Everyone. Teenagers. Middle-aged men. White-haired grandmas. Married. Single. Divorced. Everyone responds this way when he or she hears this one eyeopening thing about sex. You will too.

Got a question about sex—like whether or not it's worth waiting for, or what's acceptable when it comes to sexual expression, or whether God even cares about what happens between two consenting individuals? Or maybe you think you have it all figured out. (That's the smug place I was in when I stumbled across this life-changing truth.)

Ready to end the battle in your own soul once and for all?

This is it.

~~~~~~~~~~~~~~~~~~~~~~~~~~~~~~~~~ 3

yada. yada. yada.

it was January 2004 when I found it.

I'd been talking to larger and larger audiences about sex for several years—and I was growing bored. How many times could I say the same things about sex? Good grief! This exciting topic was becoming mundane.

My spirit just felt like there had to be something more.

Maybe you've been there, bored as you hear yet another sexual purity message drone on. Perhaps even good messages have left you wondering *why*. "Doesn't anyone else wonder *why* everyone is doing the Silver Ring Thing?" We've all heard so many trite clichés through the years. "It's a gift you can only unwrap once" and "You can become a recycled virgin" come to mind. Something in me just doesn't like the idea of comparing virginity to a milk carton. But all these repeated messages about "protecting God's gift of sex" still leave many wondering *why*! *Why* does God want it protected? Without the answer to that question, the rest of our questions about sex are difficult to address. I got to a place where I knew that answering the *why* question was critical to convincing my brothers and sisters in Christ to wait.

Here's what I did when I got to that place: I simply prayed, *God, blow me away! If I have to keep talking about this, then blow me away with something new that shows me why sex is amazing to You.*

He did.

A few weeks later, I was reading through Genesis, when I came to these seemingly innocuous words: "Adam lay with his wife Eve, and she became pregnant" (4:1). I'd read over those words before without giving them a second thought. Not this time. I caught the scent of something being not quite as it seemed. For the first time, it occurred to me: "He was *so* not just layin' there!"

Silver ring thing

Silver Ring Thing is a live event that brings students to a deeper commitment to purity by offering honest answers to real issues through a concert-style setting of comedy, drama, music, videos, and testimonies. My intent in mentioning the event in this chapter isn't to dis the organizers or participants but to give voice to the questions that movements like this sometimes prompt. In fact, I really like what they're up to and encourage you to attend an event if you are in high school or to try out for the touring team if you are in college.

Go to silverringthing.com for more details.

Clearly this was not one of Adam's more passive moments.

Sometimes the Bible makes a lot more sense if you look at it from the perspective of the original writers. So I decided to take a look.

I grabbed a Hebrew dictionary and dug through it with passion. What was the word the Hebrew writer used in that sentence? I had to know. Scanning, searching, looking...there!

There it was.

The Hebrew word for sex.

How fascinating.

Of all words!

Yada.

As in, "Yada yada yada"?

Yes!

> Adam lay [*yada*] with his wife Eve, and she became
> pregnant and gave birth to Cain.
>
> —GENESIS 4:1

You'll never hear that word the same way again. How amazingly ironic that this Hebrew word for sex[1]—a word that sends nearly everyone into laughter at some point in their lives—is most often used today to communicate a sense of boredom. Merriam-Webster.com defines it as a noun that means "boring or empty talk." "Yada yada yada" could just as well mean "blah blah blah" in our society.

Turns out it's not so boring after all.

And in Hebrew it's a verb—an action word and then some!

So what does it really mean?

The definition of the Hebrew word *yada* is "to know, to be known, to be deeply respected." What an amazing thing God thought about sex. That it was to be something that causes us to deeply know another. Without alluding directly to the physical act of sexuality, this word points to the deep emotional quenching I yearn for in the act of sex.

I'm not alone.

Almost every female I've spoken to about this admits she isn't really yearning for a physical touch in her sexual encounters but is seeking a deep emotional caressing. We want to find our guy looking at and studying us. We want to hear our name whispered. We need him to listen to our words with all his heart. We want to "be known."

ya·da

verb. to know, to be known, to be deeply respected

I really think I *began* to feel known by my husband when he was still my boyfriend. You'll probably laugh at my "eureka!" moment. You see, I'm an avid fan of hard-scooped vanilla ice cream drenched in hot fudge and topped off with bananas, nuts, and whipped cream. Not one ingredient can be omitted or substituted. (No soft serve!) One night during finals week, at about midnight, I was studying when someone knocked on my door. It was a fellow dorm resident bearing a gift for me: a perfectly crafted vanilla ice cream, hot fudge, banana, nut, and whipped cream sundae—with a note from Bob. Better than studying for his finals, my soon-to-be fiancé had been studying me. And I felt known in a way that began to draw my heart into his.

The latter part of the definition of *yada*—respect—tends to resonate with men. They want to know they have what it takes to receive your admiration. They yearn "to be deeply respected." I've asked men from my hometown of State College, Pennsylvania, to the hidden corners of Africa what they want most in a relationship. Every one of them answers, "Respect."

I've learned that I best respect my husband by affirming him and what he does. When we were in college, Bob was making money on the side selling synthetic "shammys" at flea markets. (Yep, just like the ShamWow guy! Don't be too quick to laugh. He had a ministage and sound system to demo the product, which he did in a hilarious and entertaining way. As a result, people bought his product by the armful, and he was making enough money to have several employees and buy himself a white sports car.) Introvert that I was (and am), I agreed to demo his product at the local Amish market. Something as simple as helping him sell his goods created a powerful physical and emotional drawing. He wanted me all the more because I acted in such a way that said, "I see what you do, and I respect you!"

I guess what I'm trying to say is this: hot fudge sundaes and shammys at an Amish market might not seem to have much to do with sex, based on the world's presupposition that sex is primarily physical, but an emotional knowing and deep respect are essential ingredients to an intimate, lifelong connection.

Mingle the two—an emotional knowing and a deep respect—and you have *yada*.

I can't describe it.

I won't try.

Yada!

Out of curiosity, I researched how many times this word shows up in the Hebrew Old Testament.

It's used more than nine hundred times.

Now, that's a lotta *yada*! (But you'll see as we continue exploring the word that its strength of meaning extends far beyond the marriage bed into something truly sacred.) Getting the basic definition of this word is like merely dipping your toe into the ocean of God's rich thoughts about sex. Not blown away just yet?

Hold on.

It gets even better.

4

the one thing no one ever tells you about sex

wes Alexander did not know Stephanie Buckmaster.

He first saw her at one of my Pure Freedom purity retreats for teen guys and girls. I guess you could say it was love at first sight. Before he met her, he loved her. And he made plans to win her heart.

But Stephanie's heart had been wooed by her Savior long before Wes stepped onto the scene. After a bad relationship in ninth grade, Stephanie had been called into a unique covenant with God. Prompted by the Holy Spirit through the example of a college-aged woman she met at a summer music festival, Stephanie chose to turn her eyes away from guys and toward Jesus. She felt like she needed a long gaze into the eyes of her Savior. In fact, she'd decided to do this...well, until the end of high school. Three years. No guys. Just God.

Enter Wes: "Hi, I'm Wes..." He'd barely met her and begun talking with her when she made it clear that there wasn't going to be a budding love life between them anytime soon.

Stephanie: "No offense, but I think I'm just supposed to love Jesus for the next few years."

But sparks flew. Attraction was apparent. How can you control *that*? It's not as if you plan it. It's chemical. Reactive. And apparently, combining "Wes Alexander" with a little "Stephanie Buckmaster" created fireworks. At first, he just couldn't help pursuing her.

But Wes loved Jesus too. He heard Stephanie when she said she'd made a covenant with God. So he took his attraction to his Savior. And got clear directives. During a youth conference in Orlando, Florida, Jesus told Wes that *He'd* already been courting Stephanie. God asked Wes Alexander to give His girl back.

Wes obliged. After all, it was the God of the universe asking.

to date or not to date?

In recent years, Christian teens have embraced the idea of delaying dating until they are out of high school or even older. It isn't much of a delay if you consider the dating customs around the world:

- Australia: Dating begins at age eighteen or nineteen.
- Europe: Group dating is customary during high school.
- Iran: It is against the law to date.
- Japan and Korea: Dating begins in college.[1]

For the next three years, Wes thought of Stephanie, watched her from afar, stayed close as a friend, and prayed. During this time, he was often asked out by girls. It was easy for him to rebuff them. They just weren't his true love—the one God had said Wes could pursue *after* she graduated from high school.

They saw each other again on May 24, 2008, just before she graduated. Three years had passed since he'd first laid eyes on her. Nearly ten months had gone by since they'd even seen each other. None of the desire had faded.

Then Wes came to see her on June 1, 2008.

That's when he brought them out. The gifts.

One for each Christmas that he'd loved her.

One for each birthday.

And a journal that expressed his emotional pursuit of her heart, tempered by the trust Wes had to exercise by putting his hopes in God's hands. Three years of seeking her heart was laid bare in the gifts he chose and the words he wrote.

The rest is history.

———————

That's what I'm talkin' about! That is the kind of love every girl dreams of. And it's the kind of love that foreshadows *yada*.

You see, *yada* is characterized by a *seeking*. Before there can be *yada*, there must be a quest. A faithful, long-term search.[2] The quest of a heart propelled by true love, not selfish desire. Think of it as "before love." *Before love* is a yearning and searching for someone who does not yet reciprocate that love.

Wes loved Stephanie before she loved him. Before she had met him. And that brings me to the true power of the word *yada*—and the one thing no one ever tells you.

You'll recall that our precious word is used more than nine hundred times in the Old Testament. We started with Genesis 4:1: "Adam lay [*yada*] with his wife Eve, and she became pregnant and gave birth to Cain." Here are a few similar passages:

> Cain lay [*yada*] with his wife, and she became pregnant and gave birth to Enoch.
>
> —GENESIS 4:17

> Adam lay [*yada*] with his wife again, and she gave birth to a son and named him Seth.
>
> —GENESIS 4:25

> [Rebekah] was very beautiful, a virgin; no man had ever lain [*yada*] with her.
>
> —GENESIS 24:16

> Early the next morning they arose and worshiped before the LORD and then went back to their home at Ramah. Elkanah lay [*yada*] with Hannah his wife, and the LORD remembered her. So in the course of time Hannah conceived and gave birth to a son. She named him Samuel, saying, "Because I asked the LORD for him."
>
> —1 SAMUEL 1:19-20

There are several other times when the word is used like this, to convey a deep emotional knowing and mutual respect between a naked man and wife. But we've got a long way to go to find the more than nine hundred times the word is used. And here's where my study started to blow me away. Are you ready? The word *yada* is used most commonly in verses like this:

> Be still, and know [*yada*] that I am God.
>
> —PSALM 46:10
>
> So the LORD said to Moses, "I will also do this thing that you have spoken; for you have found grace in My sight, and I know [*yada*] you by name."
>
> —EXODUS 33:17, NKJV
>
> But since then there has not arisen in Israel a prophet like Moses, whom the LORD knew [*yada*] face to face.
>
> —DEUTERONOMY 34:10, NKJV

It's clear from these verses that *yada* isn't about a merely physical act. Rather, *yada* is a word of intimacy that transcends the physical. It describes the whole knowing of a person. It portrays an uncovering and an embrace of the nakedness of another. There are no secrets and nothing is held back.

Such is the love we are called to know with God through Christ Jesus our Lord. Do you know that kind of love with God? If you don't, you can be sure He is seeking you.

O LORD, you have searched me
    and you know [*yada*] me.
You know [*yada*] when I sit and when I rise;
    you perceive my thoughts from afar.
You discern my going out and my lying down;
    you are familiar with all my ways.
Before a word is on my tongue
    you know [*yada*] it completely, O LORD....

For you created my inmost being;
    you knit me together in my mother's womb.
I praise you because I am fearfully and wonderfully
        made;
    your works are wonderful,
    I know [*yada*] that full well.
My frame was not hidden from you
    when I was made in the secret place.
    When I was woven together in the depths
        of the earth,
your eyes saw my unformed body.
    All the days ordained for me
    were written in your book
    before one of them came to be....

Search me, O God, and know [*yada*] my heart.

—PSALM 139:1–4, 13–16, 23

Just as a young romantic dreams of his or her future lover, God dreamed of you. Before you were born, His heart longed for you. God has "before love" for you. He *has* sought you, and He *is* seeking you. Those are facts. Let's make every effort not to confuse our lack of feeling God's presence with a lack of His presence. And beyond that, my friend, let me encourage you to step out of—or never to step into—the same pit of Satan's lies I once was drowning in when I believed that my past made me unworthy of God's desire and love. It's simply not true. In fact, His relentless seeking of us is clearly stated in Scripture: Where can we go from His Spirit? Where can we flee from His presence?[3] Malcolm Smith writes,

> Now, in this moment, you are the focus of the passionate and unconditional love of God. He loves you with His entire Being. You have all of His love as if you were the only human in existence. And He loves you because you exist without reference to your behavior. Understand and live in that reality, and behavior will change in response to such infinite love that leaves us worshipping in wonder. As John says, "We love, because He first loved us" (1 John 4:19, NASB).[4]

Get this: The ache in your heart to be known by and to truly know one man was placed in you to be a revelation of a much deeper love. When you are in intimate physical and emotional communion with your husband, it will be a mere picture of the passionate love of a God who has been seeking your heart since before you were born.

Perhaps you've been seeking too—but somehow you missed hearing Him call your name. A lot of counterfeit loves lurk out there.

After all, just as you have a Hero fervently seeking your heart, a Villain is eager to stomp on your soul. He will stop at nothing to see the picture of God's great love destroyed in your life. The Villain will woo you starting in kindergarten with seemingly innocent boyfriends, will magnify your dad's weaknesses so you hate men, will put a microphone up to your parents' mouths when their relationship is struggling so you'll hate marriage, will lure you into sexting, and will carelessly trample on your virginity and then tell you that you are used goods. He doesn't play fair. He introduces lies and counterfeits to us in every shape and form. He will do his absolute worst to rub out the true picture of God's love in your life.

So we keep seeking.

Searching for God.

Searching for true human love.

> The *ultimate* reason (not the only one) why we are sexual is to make God more deeply knowable.
>
> —John Piper[5]

Not realizing that they are intimately connected. Not certain of what's counterfeit and what's real. It's been so long since our hearts— since the church's heart—have been familiar with what intimate love is supposed to look like. So, time and again, our God keeps pointing us back to His kind of love...to *yada*.

This is the one thing no one has ever told you about sex: it's an exquisite revelation of a much Greater Love.

As God looks upon humanity, groaning to communicate His love, He wants to direct our attention to a portrait that comes close to helping us understand. That portrait is a pure, holy marriage. In that sacred place alone do we find a taste of the intimacy we can have with a living, loving God.

But the picture has not been treasured as the masterpiece it is. We have to look hard under the careless vandalism of culture to catch a glimpse of the original brush strokes. Maybe that's why the word *yada* can be traced from Genesis to Revelation. So God can remind us of what true intimacy looks like.

He has to.

We keep wandering so far.

not all sex is the same

when you are on to something in the Bible, keep reading. I did when I first found the word *yada*.

And I came across something quite chilling.

Go with me to one of the most sordid accounts in the Holy Scriptures. In Genesis 19, Lot and his daughters have just left Sodom and Gomorrah, cities known for their decadence and sin. The Bible says God destroyed them with burning sulfur. Lot's wife held too tightly to the cities and fell behind. The Bible says she became a pillar of salt, probably not unlike those images of frozen terror we see remaining in the ancient ruins of Pompeii.

Beyond being homeless and motherless, Lot and his daughters face another problem.

No sons.

How will the family name be carried on? Are the young women destined to become old maids? After their father dies, who will care for them in a male-dominated society where women are dependent on male relatives?

The older daughter decides to take the situation into her own hands. This is where the story becomes detestable. She gets her father drunk and then...well, this is a little too gross for me to put into words. Let's stick with exactly what's recorded in the Bible. She "went in and lay with him" (Genesis 19:33).

Now, you should be reacting at this point because this is disgusting. When I first read the story in the context of *yada,* on top of my difficulty fathoming this twisted act of incest, I found myself grieving at what seemed to be a familiar word. Could this word *lay,* used here to describe a horrid act of depravity, be the same beautiful Hebrew word I'd discovered earlier—*yada?*

I reached once again for my Hebrew language aids.

Scanning the pages hopefully, I soon found what I was looking for.

I was thankful to discover that *shakab*—not *yada*—is the Hebrew word used in this instance for "lay."

In my *Key Word Study Bible,* the word *shakab*[1] is described as a "euphemism of sexual intercourse."[2] It's often paired with the word *sikba,* which means "emission." So basically, *shakab* means "to exchange body fluids."

When I share this with a live audience, an audible gag reflex often rumbles through the masses.

This is a grotesque description of sex.

Some sex is God's sex. It's *yada.*

Some sex is a mere counterfeit. It's *shakab.*

I think that's why so many people who are sexually active outside of marriage find it unfulfilling. In *Sex and the Soul,* by Boston University's Donna Freitas, 41 percent of sexually active college students used these words to describe last night's hookup: "awkward, used, dirty, empty, regretful, ashamed, alone, miserable, disgusted, duped…"[3] I could go on. Maybe it wasn't really sex at all. Just an exchange of body fluids.

As I was writing this book, I took advantage of the fact that I live in the hometown of Penn State University (a little shout-out to my fellow Nittany Lions fans!). To say that the campus is a breeding ground (no pun intended) for sexual promiscuity is an understatement. I like the place. It has its good qualities, but encouraging self-control within the student body is not one of them. Rather, Penn State is known as one of the nation's most intoxicated campuses, which inevitably results in a lot of sex.

I've spent a little bit of time talking to women on campus. One of them, Clarisse, was raised in a strong Christian home and was home-schooled until high school. Now she's had more sex partners than she can remember. (I mean that. It's not a cliché. She and I tried to count them up. We couldn't.) We met up at the HUB, the school's gathering center and eatery, and decided on two slices of pepperoni pizza and a couple of root beers to flavor our conversation.

"In high school, I did it to be popular. That's what popular girls do," she said about her decision to start having sex. "The first time was so stupid. It was meaningless. I so regret doing it." (There's one of Freitas's words: regret.)

"In college, it just *is*." She described the culture of sex on campus. "It's what everyone does. It's the *norm*."

At Penn State, on any day in almost any class, you can hear about the previous night's conquests in the jabbering of students as they find their seats. Boastful stories of sexual exploits in humorous and graphic play-by-play detail provide as much perk as the caffeine in each student's grip. It's presented as the most common kind of recreational fun among students.

But for Clarisse, the pleasure has dissolved into pain.

"You tell yourself it's just physical. That you won't feel it," she said, referring to any emotion regarding sex. "But you eventually do. And then it hurts."

She's decided to not be sexually active right now, as she classifies herself as "confused."

"I've taken the Walk of Shame," she said, leaning in to whisper her confession. She nibbled on her pizza crust pensively, her big eyes misting with tears. The Walk of Shame, if you haven't heard, is the telltale evidence of sex on campus. It happens around noon, when everyone else is in sweats and tees. A lone girl—hair tousled and miniskirt wrinkled—wobbles across campus in heels she slipped into the previous evening.

"Even if you just stay at a girlfriend's apartment the night before, you don't want to walk around like that," explained Clarisse. "It says something bad about you. Like you're easy." I gather from her comment that even the girl with more sexual partners than she can count doesn't want to be seen as easy.

Then her tears cleared and a fiery anger came into her eyes.

"What I can't get over is this." She paused for emphasis. "When a guy does it, they call it the Walk of Fame."

No wonder she's confused.

Sex can never be reduced to something purely physical. Eventually your emotions will catch up. For Clarisse, they caught up while she was still in college. For Antonia, another young woman I talked to, reality hit at a much less convenient time.

Fresh from her honeymoon, Antonia agreed to meet me for coffee on the campus where she'd spent four years of her life. I sat across from her, one of the most perfect creatures you'll ever meet. Flawless tanned skin, high cheekbones, and full lips give her a look that belongs in Hollywood. She's the reason other women get plastic surgery. The perfect complement to her exquisite features is a saucy Hispanic accent.

"I had my first drink in college," reported Antonia, who lived with her Christian mom until she came to Penn State. She described her life up to that point as somewhat sheltered. That all changed soon after her arrival at college. "I was introduced to clubbing and sleeping around here on this campus." Friends pressed her to go clubbing, then

Internet dating

Approximately 29 percent of eighteen- to twenty-five-year-old women are logging on to find Mr. Right.[4] Dating sites, once the fodder of seedy conversation, are mainstream fare for the single girl. Are they bad? Not necessarily. I have several happily married friends who met online!

But be selective. A "dating" site might actually attract guys who aren't interested in the party scene and who are looking for commitment, but it is not a guarantee. And if you go to one of the sites that feature religious affiliation and spiritual interest, you might be able to find a guy who has the right ingredient in his life—Jesus—to be a good life partner.

to drink just a little, then a lot. Before she knew it, she was joining in with not just the drinking but the sex too.

Antonia had only one sexual partner, never took the Walk of Shame, and had a really great church community to help her heal. But she didn't recognize the extent of the damage done...until the day she got back from her honeymoon. (Can you say "unfortunate timing"?)

"We got back from this perfect honeymoon, and I was plagued with guilt and unworthiness," she said. She couldn't help comparing the new and pure passion of physical intimacy with her loving and forgiving husband to the more sordid sex she'd had with a guy she's now estranged from—and the comparison resulted in more emotional conflict over her sin than she'd known was possible. She glanced off into the distance, her eyes telling the story of memories she wishes she didn't have. "It's sad to come home and to know right away that your marriage is already wounded by something stupid you did."

She sighed. "We have a lot of work to do," she said quietly.

At a time when she should be reveling in the freedom to enjoy her new marriage bed, Antonia is learning how much work it will take to do that. Many women who are sexually active as teens find themselves either emotionally or physically challenged by intimacy once they are married. I counsel them every day. For the sake of transparency, I will tell you that I have been one of them—and sometimes I still struggle in this area!

You can try to reduce sex to a simple exchange of body fluids and treat it casually, but reality will catch up with you. (I'll show you in the next chapter how your body chemistry cannot possibly handle casual sex in the way the world advocates.) Treating sex solely as a physical act has disastrous consequences that our culture rarely acknowledges in its careless approach to female sexuality.

Consider the evolution of Miley Cyrus. One day she's Hannah Montana, the girl your little sister watches on a Disney sitcom. The next day she's dressed like a sexy bird, sporting a twenty-thousand-dollar bustier and selling her body for the world. While her "Can't Be Tamed" video is mild compared to the antics of Christina Aguilera and Lady Gaga, it displays violent sexual imagery and hints at self-pleasuring. Why? Because apparently in our culture, you're not a real star until you've done something shockingly sexual.

> Every man who knocks on the door of a brothel is looking for God.
>
> —G. K. Chesterton

The Mileys, Britneys, and Beyoncés of the world are rewarded for acting like tramps. They make millions of dollars for their shocking shenanigans. But if *you* act like a tramp, you'll be trashed and find yourself taking the Walk of Shame, not the Walk of Fame.

Why?

Because what our culture sells us is not real sex. It's not *yada*. It's *shakab*. While it does offer sometimes-potent pleasure, it always falls short of ultimate fulfillment. The pinnacle of sexual pleasure comes only in God's perfect design of *yada*. I hope to prove that to you as we continue exploring God's heart for your sexuality.

Maybe you know all too well what I'm talking about. Perhaps you've chased down every sexual conquest possible, only to realize you still haven't found what you're looking for.

Engaging physically in sexual behavior isn't the only way to water down your passion for true, intimate, *yada* sex. While I was writing this book, sexting was the counterfeit of choice for at least one outspoken, prominent Christian woman: former Miss California Carrie Prejean. Perhaps you are addicted to erotic novels or pornography. Did you know that young women who expose themselves to these fake sexual and romantic loves tend to lose their appetite for a real relationship?

Perhaps this is best seen in the zombielike way girls approach their romantic worship of a fictional vampire named Edward Cullen. Here's what one girl wrote online:

> okay, twilight has seriously distorted my view on guys! i'm
> going to be single forever because i'm waiting for edward, who,
> as we all know, doesn't exactly exist. O_O -cries- EDWARD!
> i'm going to have to settle for a guy who isn't immortal and a
> vampire. :([5]

Sadly, her comment echoes the unfulfilled longings of hundreds of thousands of hearts. And it's going to have an impact. I'm not talking about the girl who enjoys reading or watching *Twilight*. I'm talking about the girl who becomes obsessed with it, as so many have. The counterfeit tends to consume them to such an extent mentally and physically that they lose their fullest desire for an actual physical relationship. [6]

You can't pursue impersonal forms of romance without it having an impact. Even the secular world can see this. A 2009 article detailing the results of a survey of eleven hundred *Self* magazine readers—61 percent of whom reported viewing porn on their computer—warned that if you like having sex with a mate, you should probably push pause on the porn. (It also noted that it can be a real depressor in terms of your own body image.) This freethinking writer suggested at least cutting back on porn viewing.[7]

Even those who promote the premise of no-strings-attached sex recognize that somewhere along the way our culture has taken things too far. We've robbed ourselves of something real to chase after a mere counterfeit.

Know this: Not all sex is the same. Some acts of sexuality reflect the deep knowing and mutual respecting God intended.

Others are nothing more than a physical act.

And that's just not enough.

friends with benefits

i have a confession to make.

As a little girl, I often fell asleep dreaming of romance.

Not of sex or temptation or playful lovers' antics, but of beautiful, action-packed romance. That my hero fought a courageous battle to rescue me went without saying. Visions of my own vulnerable capture by an evil force were followed by a triumphant clashing of swords and my being carried off into the sunset. Just before I fell asleep, I would take the extra pillow in my bed, turn it to vertically line up with my body, and rest my head in the protective nook of my dreamed-of hero's "shoulder."

Don't laugh! You probably did it too, huh? The Pillow Partner. Perfect in every way.

Why on God's green earth did we do that?

Because deep inside us is that craving to know and be known—to experience *yada*.

The *Theological Lexicon of the Old Testament* devotes pages and pages to unfolding the veiled meaning and depth of the Hebrew word. Along with implying access and nearness to the object being "known," the concept of *yada* includes something odd. You see, even though we must be physically close to "know" one another, the word suggests that the knowing doesn't come through our physical senses. It takes more than taste, touch, and vision to experience *yada*. In its fullest meaning, the word emphasizes "the role that the 'heart' plays as an organ of perception."[1] In other words, *yada* is emotional!

And here's where the humanistic worldview of sexuality breaks down.

The sexual revolution of the sixties and seventies—birthed (ironically) in part by the Pill, which took away the "inconvenience" of pregnancy—sought to define sex under the premise that you and I are merely mammals. Since animals have sex solely because of an instinctual drive toward pleasure (which nicely results in reproduction), surely our sexual behavior should be viewed as nothing more than a mammalian pursuit of pleasure (and how masterful that we have learned to control the complicating side effect of reproduction). The physical senses alone drive our behavior. If it feels good, do it.

I doubt the pioneers of the movement could've ever imagined just how far it would go. Cruising along the New Millennium highway, we've driven those sexual revolution Volkswagen hippie vans into entirely new territory. We call it "friends with benefits." Since it's all about just our physical senses, there's no need to get our emotions involved in the act of sex. If you're feeling hot, call up a friend and arrange for a hookup. No strings attached.

Warthogs aren't limited by morals.

Why should we be?

But it doesn't work. Even those shaped by this animalistic view of the human sex drive have found that it has some flaws. Take the beautiful and talented actress Kate Hudson, who claims to embrace this worldview of sex. She says,

> I don't think we're made up to be monogamous: we are animals.

Despite her declared certainty, she's confused.

> That said, I could never be in a relationship that wasn't monogamous...I couldn't deal with it. There is something sacred about the relationship that is broken.[2]

As I heard San Diego pastor Ted Hamilton so eloquently phrase it, "She's pulled toward monogamy, even though she doesn't believe in monogamy."[3]

Why?

I know why. Her brain was created for monogamy. Friend, let me introduce you to your deep limbic system.

The deep limbic system is the part of the brain that stores and classifies odor, music, symbols, and memory. Sounds like a recipe for romance when you think of it in terms of a good splash of cologne on your guy's neck, an iPod playlist downloaded in the name of romance, and a bouquet of red roses.

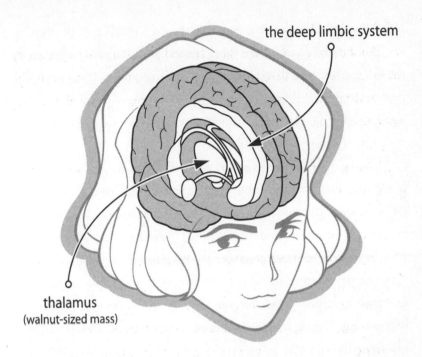

the deep limbic system

thalamus
(walnut-sized mass)

You see, the brain chemicals associated with sex wash over the deep limbic system during a wide variety of romantic experiences. Holding hands, smelling your guy, listening to music, embracing, a gentle massage, and most powerfully, the act of sexual intercourse work together to create a cocktail of chemicals that records memories deep in the emotional center of your brain. (That's why we remember sexual experiences and images so clearly.)

One of the critical neurochemicals released during sex is dopamine. Dopamine makes you feel good; it creates a simultaneous sense of peace and pleasure. Anytime your body experiences pleasure— whether morally "good" or "bad"—the limbic system gets washed in dopamine. In essence, it is the "craving" chemical. It makes you want more. It creates addiction. This can be an addiction to working out or to having sex with your spouse. It can also be an addiction to smoking or porn. Neurochemicals are value-neutral and don't care whether it's marital sex or crystal meth making you feel good. They wash the brain's receptors anytime the body feels pleasure.

Dopamine emotionally "attaches" you to the source of pleasure— even if that source is "just a friend."

Can you see how this is part of God's plan for sex within marriage? He put it in black and white when He inspired these words: "The two will become one flesh" (Ephesians 5:31). While a man and woman's "oneness" extends beyond the physical, the evidence suggests that God designed our emotional headquarters to be made "one" through the physical act of sex. We become, in a sense, addicted to our marriage bed! Why? Because God designed our emotional system for one lifelong, mutually monogamous relationship. (I call that marriage!)

But what happens if you get caught up in a sexual relationship— or several—when you're fifteen or sixteen or twenty? What happens when you play the "friends with benefits" game? What happens when the guy your brain has become "addicted to" is gone? You experience withdrawal symptoms in the emotional center of the brain (translation: your heart hurts).

The limbic system was created to store sexual memory and emotion for us. A little walnut-sized mass called the thalamus—not the big blood-pumping organ one foot below it—is the seat of our romantic "heart." The purpose of the limbic system and dopamine is to turn the visceral drives of passion into a deep, lasting attachment—into knowing and being known. But when this gets misused, our system becomes confused and we feel great pain.

I felt this pain deeply in my young adult years. While I never endured any physical consequences for my sexual sin, I knew all too well the emotional pain of it. I would awaken every single day in college and feel like there was just something wrong, and then I'd remember. "Oh, yeah. *That!*" It was at the center of my mind so much of the time—before I broke up with the guy (thinking we'd have to stay together no matter what because of the sex) and after (wondering why it hurt so much). In all, about ten years of my life were characterized by deep sexual pain, caused mostly by ripping apart a connection superglued with dopamine.

Memory and love

The memory of our lovers' perfume may linger long after their more easily verbalized telephone numbers have faded forever.... I recall a woman incapacitated by Alzheimer's who, upon hearing a certain man's name—dead for fifty years—exclaimed, "Oh, John, I was once very much in love with him!"

—George Vaillant[4]

One of the college women I spoke to was altering her entire life plans because of the glue created in her sexual relationship. Taylor, a strong-willed, brilliant girl, had experienced two sexual relationships. She admitted that she and the first guy were "just friends." She didn't mean to like him so much.

"I couldn't get over him," she said. "I'm still not totally over it."

Then she told me how the new guy became part of the picture before the first guy was out. After all, the first guy was just a friend, while the new guy seemed emotionally interested. As she talked, it was hard for me to believe that Taylor couldn't see that she'd essentially used the new relationship as a mild painkiller to numb the agony of ending the sexual connection in the first "friendship."

"I feel *tied*," she said. She actually said it. She used the word *tied*. Then she went on to explain that she has a really cool call of God on her life but that she's afraid she won't follow it. "This guy wants me to follow him," she explained about the new guy and his plan for her to move out of the country with him.

And she probably will follow this guy because she's addicted to him.

We were created to be addicted—glued—to the person we have sex with. But just to one. And not until we're committed by a marriage covenant. Or our hearts get hurt.

That's because true sex—*yada*—as theologian Claus Westermann describes it, is "the bodily relationship of man and woman...not thought of primarily as physiological, but as personal." It's heart-driven sex. Westermann notes that, in Scripture, the word *yada* is used only in the sense of humans and not of animals.[5] The Bible says human sex is different from the sex of a warthog. It's not just instinctual.

The Wounds of *Shakab*

To embrace the Bible's definition of true sex is to understand that the physical act of sex is meant to deepen one's heart perception of knowing and being known. In the Garden of Eden, Adam and Eve were naked but "felt no shame" (Genesis 2:25). This nakedness went far beyond his buff body and her curvaceous beauty. They were exposed to each other in every way. There was no desire to keep secrets or cover up. There were no deceptions, heartless manipulations, or dating games.

Just shameless oneness between one man and one woman.

The sexual revolution didn't bring that. Turns out, simply exchanging body fluids (even when it's with a friend) actually hurts a lot.

I'm not talking about physical pain but emotional pain. For all the emotional pleasure God meant for us to know in the context of *yada*, I've spent a large part of my adult life picking up the pieces of girls who have been deeply wounded by sexual pain known in the context of *shakab*.

After a speaking engagement, I was driven to the airport by a beautiful Southern belle we'll call Madison. She told me how for five years she'd dated a guy who was as committed to purity as she was, and after they broke up they were still good friends. She said that they were deeply emotionally connected at one point, but God had enabled them to go their separate ways without a lot of pain. Then she dated a guy for six months. They were barely more than friends, certainly not emotionally committed to each other. He didn't share her resolve for purity, and over time he broke her down. She didn't give him much. He just got under her shirt. Through tears she said, "He just touched my breasts. That's it. But why, pleeease tell me why, a relationship that lasted five years can not hurt at all, but one that lasted only six months can cut through to the very core of me and split me up?"

We prayed and talked. And I was certain Madison was going to be okay. While she had clearly experienced a great measure of brokenness by letting her guard down, I was able to encourage her about how much of herself she still had to give to her future husband. After some time, she realized that facing the pain caused by sexual contact, which by today's standards was mild, could become her strength of resolve to pursue purity again. She left me at the US Airways departure gate with a big smile of determination!

But some of the girls I've prayed with through the years have not been okay with so little counseling. Instead, they have needed months or years of more intense help. I've served as something of a triage center, directing them to local churches and counseling services that could help them to heal. The sexual encounters (*shakab*) in their lives had left them hollow and broken. These girls had been having fun in the moment. They weren't abused or forced. They liked the physical act of sex, but when the guys were gone and the high from the brain chemicals wore off, they were left with the sober reality that they'd been used. The aftermath was deep depression and often suicidal tendencies. (Did you know that sexually active teens are more likely to attempt suicide than their virgin peers?)[6]

friends with benefits defined

UrbanDictionary.com defines *friends with benefits* as "two friends who have a sexual relationship without being emotionally involved." One day a girl calls up a guy friend because she feels like fooling around. The invitation is extended to hook up. No strings attached. But then, those chemicals kick in during the sex. Now she's feeling a little bit, well, addicted to her guy friend. What comes next? You do the science. (Don't forget the dopamine!)

The impact didn't end there. Some hated men. (Ironic, is it not, how giving yourself carelessly to guys can create hatred for them.) Some hated themselves and, specifically, their bodies. (The American Psychological Association links early sexual activity by girls with an inability to enjoy a healthy adult sexual life and points to a great preoccupation with and dislike for their bodies.[7]) Some who'd messed around with oral sex and mutual masturbation—saving the actual climax for marriage—couldn't have orgasms when they finally did get married (they'd trained their bodies to get to a certain point and stop, and it did). I could go on.

Many of them have posed the same question Madison did: why does it hurt so much?

Why Does Sex Outside of Marriage Hurt So Much?

After counseling hundreds of deeply wounded girls, I have no doubt in my mind that a chemical bond is created between you and any person you have sex with—whether you consider the relationship nothing more than a friendship or whether you have been deeply emotionally connected. There's no way around it. Having sex bonds you to each other. Some people call these "soul ties." Perhaps that's why the apostle Paul warned us, "Do you not know that he who unites himself with a prostitute is one with her in body? For it is said, 'The two will become one flesh'" (1 Corinthians 6:16).

Lauren Winner, author of *Real Sex*, says Paul is really writing, "Don't you know that when you sleep with someone, your body makes a promise whether you do or not?"[8]

I guess the bottom line is this: we aren't animals. True sex was created to be a deep emotional connection, not an instinctual urge to be accommodated every time you feel sexy. That's why you and I are going to build a sexual theology to drive your love life. It doesn't mean your body and your emotions won't *try* to drive. But, hopefully, as you embrace God's truth about sex, your body and emotions will take a backseat until your head—and God's Spirit—gives you the green light of a wedding day to know and be known.

Friends with benefits?

Now there's a paradox of mutual exclusivity. Despite the desire to remove emotion and commitment, the act of sex guarantees that your emotions will be invited into the relationship and you'll no longer be "just friends."

There's no way to short-circuit the God-designed connection between sex and your heart.

relational love

a s k little boys and little girls about each other, and you're
sure to hear some crazy ideas about love. Take, for example, these true
thoughts on kissing:[1]

> You learn [how to kiss] right on the spot when the gooshy
> feelings get the best of you. ——DOUG, AGE 7
>
> I know one reason kissing was created. It makes you feel
> warm all over, and they didn't always have electric heat or
> fireplaces or even stoves in their houses. ——GINA, AGE 8
>
> The rules goes like this: if you kiss someone, then you
> should marry her and have kids with her. It's the right
> thing to do. ——HOWARD, AGE 8
>
> Never kiss in front of other people. It's a big embarrassing
> thing if anybody sees you. But if nobody sees you, I might
> be willing to try it with a handsome boy, but just for a few
> hours. ——KALLY, AGE 9

How naive our young minds can be about love. But, on the other hand, at least these kids recognize that girls like to kiss boys and vice versa. Sadly, as we grew up, many of us forgot why girls are girls and boys are boys and why they sometimes like to kiss.

Let's go back to the Garden of Eden.

Adam and Eve Are Statues

"In the beginning God created" (Genesis 1:1). Distinct in this creation were Adam and Eve. The pinnacle of God's design, they were created to represent something greater.

> Then God said, "Let Us make man in Our image, according to Our likeness...." So God created man in His own image; in the image of God He created him; male and female He created them.
>
> —GENESIS 1:26–27, NKJV

We—male and female—are the image or likeness of God. Why doesn't God mention the traits of being intelligent or worshipful or creative when He says we were created in His image? Why doesn't He commend our language proficiency or our ability to compose sonnets? Apparently these are not the only things that make us a representation of God's image. And perhaps they aren't the most important qualities. Maybe there's one that trumps the rest.

The Bible mentions only gender in reference to our divine design. Maleness.

Femaleness.

Why? Because the one true God is a social being. This nature is clearly seen in the Trinity. God the Father, God the Son, and God the Holy Spirit—though distinctly separate—exist together in perfect and constant communion with one another. And the unique distinction between maleness and femaleness invites us to be social beings too. Our male and female differences are what create our craving for *yada*. We wouldn't long to be known if we were all alike, right? The experience of being known means we start at a place of being *unknown*. This places authentic humanity and sexuality in the context of male and female diversity.

To respond to the confusing gender messages around us, we have to go back to the beginning and ask, what is human?

As we saw in the previous chapter, the secular sexual worldview declares that to be human is to be an animal and, therefore, we can follow any physical or instinctual urges we might have. But a biblical worldview tells us that to be human is to be—as a distinct female or male—the image of God. His "statue." When people look at us, they see Him.

That's pretty holy.

Any other view of gender is little more than one of the Villain's battlegrounds for eliminating our belief in the existence of God.

Celebrating Diversity

Everywhere I go, it seems, I am inundated with posters and ads celebrating diversity. But I rarely find a celebration of the diversity found in maleness and femaleness. Why isn't that worth celebration?

Actor Rob Lowe, with no claims to be a theologian, hit the nail on the head when he said,

> I enjoy women and celebrate their differences from men. It's what makes life interesting. Women want to be listened to. Men want to feel supported by women. We're very different. I discovered that when I married.[2]

Do you see what I see? He said that women want to be listened to (*known*) and men want to feel supported (*respected*).

be wary of a Mystical approach to sex

The practices of Tantra, Taoism, and *Kama Sutra* are expressions of a sexual theology built upon cosmic humanism. This worldview, deeply influenced by ancient Eastern religions, promises great physical pleasure on the way to spiritual enlightenment, culminating in a godlikeness for the pursued and the pursuer. This is quite pragmatic and empowering for, say, a prostitute who can now characterize herself as a goddess or a spiritual therapist as she services her clients with a "healing touch."

This may seem far removed from our world, but a spring 2010 *Oprah* episode featured a sex therapist who prescribed Tantric yoga as a therapy for couples who needed help with their sex lives. While what was shown was mild, I really believe that Tantric yoga can eventually lead to spiritual

Yada.

To know. To be known. To be deeply respected.

It is the very fact of our differences that beckons us to the search, to the pursuit of knowing. Without variations to explore, there's no mystery and the desire to search is suffocated. These differences aren't rocket science.

As Lowe points out, there are obvious emotional differences. Might I invite you to grab a cuppa and review the whole deep limbic system thing from chapter 6? *Vive la différence!*

You see, both male and female brains have a deep limbic system—

bondage. It often begins as an innocent quest for sexual pleasure, but it is always headed toward connection with darkness. Those deeply involved in the movement claim to have found a "familiar spirit" or "spirit guide." The Bible teaches that such entities are demonic.

Yet many people claim that a mystical approach to sex poses no contradiction to the Christian faith. One author states, "You do not need to renounce your current religion to practice Tantra. Ideally, Tantra should enhance your established beliefs, not replace them."[3] And I find that more and more Christians are dabbling in this stuff.

This shift toward combining Eastern mysticism with sex is not new; in fact, it's a return to something old: paganism. As my friend Peter Jones points out in *The God of Sex,* "The pagan religions of ancient Canaan maintain a similar view of spirituality and sexuality."[4] It's not progress. It's regression.

that emotional headquarters for our heart. Both experience that addictive love chemical, dopamine. But, girlfriend, our emotional headquarters are two to three times larger than the average guy's, even though guys typically have larger brains overall. You and I are wired to be emotional! We have more brain real estate to fill up with smell, taste, touch, and memory.

Our brain structure explains some of our emotional differences.[5] While some men are more verbal and emotional, as a general rule men are not as great as women at interpreting facial expressions, expressing their feelings, and understanding yours. (Which is why when you are in a serious relationship, you constantly have to say, "I think we should talk." And you do, and then you feel great, and then you don't talk, so you don't feel great, so you need to say, "I think we should talk" again. And so the cycle goes.) As a woman, you are *emotionally unique* from guys.

Then there are the obvious visual differences. *The Office's* John Krasinski says,

> I've always been a fan of a girl's waist. I love that contour where it starts breaking into a little slope downwards.[6]

Cute. Romantic.
The Wire's Dominic West says,

> I like curvy women. I think most men do.[7]

We are curvy. Guys are boxy. And they weigh, on average, thirty pounds more than we do. Whether you have a cute kiwi-sized A-cup bra in your drawer or a supportive coconut-sized F-cup bra hanging in the closet, you are *visually unique* from any male ever born.

There are obvious functional differences. In general, men are more active and athletic. My husband survived a Jet Ski accident that ripped his pelvis into two pieces. The only thing holding him together was skin. I also have a photograph of him wrestling a bull with his bare hands, which he later admitted might not have been the smartest thing he's ever done. I prefer a nice bubble bath and a good book for entertainment. Much safer!

Men are biologically wired to be risk takers and to be more spatially coordinated. That tends to make them better at sports. But if you're like my friend Suzy, you might have developed that part of your brain over the years—which is possible—to be competitive on the same playing field!

As women, we are uniquely capable of incubating life created in a one-man/one-woman relationship. I have never met a guy who gets cramps. I've never met a man who could incubate a fertilized egg and grow a baby in his womb. This, despite the fact that in 2008, Oprah celebrated a "man" who gave birth. Great controversy surrounded the birth, and many condemned the fact that pregnant Thomas Beatie, who had a breast reduction to become "male" but did not have reconstructive genital surgery, was still female. But Oprah encouraged the couple, saying, "I can't imagine fifty years from now—however people choose to live—with harmony. I don't think people will be judging it…and I applaud you."[8] I tend to side with the public outcry that the "man" was functionally female, making this not much of a miracle.

So no matter how our culture tries to obscure reality, as a woman you are *functionally unique* from every man ever born.

All of this diversity between male and female is necessary to oneness. The human capacity for true oneness between two people is directly related to each person's degree of differentiation from the other. The differences enable us to emotionally, physically, and functionally *fit into* and *complete* one another.

The Echo of *Echad*

The male and the female are two distinct, independent humans, but when they come together, they are one, or in the Hebrew, *echad*.

> For this reason a man will leave his father and mother and be united to his wife, and they will become one [*echad*] flesh.
>
> —GENESIS 2:24

The Hebrew word *echad*—used here to describe the connection between distinct maleness and femaleness—echoes the greater unity represented within marriage. An ancient Jewish prayer found in the book of Deuteronomy cries out,

> Hear, O Israel: The LORD our God, the LORD is one [*echad*].
>
> —DEUTERONOMY 6:4

You see, God is distinctly three (Father, Son, Spirit), and yet in divine communion He is *echad*. Bob and I are distinctly two, but when we are joined together and in fellowship with each other and God, we are *echad*. I believe God chose maleness and femaleness as His likeness because He is a relational being.

Coming together makes us *echad*.

And that makes sex spiritual.

It is not spiritual in a mystical, New Age kind of way. Beware of the backlash against the dissatisfaction created by the sexual revolution, which defined humankind as mammals and invited sexual behavior for the purpose of pleasure alone. To counteract the emptiness

Philematology facts

Philematology is the scientific name for kissing! Here are some crazy facts for you to think about the next time you pucker up (or the first):

- A kiss quickens your pulse to one hundred beats a minute.
- A soft little kiss burns three calories.
- Men who kiss their wives every morning before work live an average of five years longer than men who don't!
- In Connecticut, it actually used to be illegal for a husband to kiss his wife on Sunday.
- Inarguably, the sweetest kiss in a film was between Lady and the Tramp. (It was also the sauciest!)

found in free sex, some are advocating that we direct our sexual desires toward the mystical qualities found in expressions of cosmic humanism. These proponents of "spiritual sex" attempt to define man as god, as they view all of the universe as a part of god.

I'm no more a god than I am a blue-footed booby (a bird). I am human. As such, I am a statue of the One True God, and my sexuality is a significant part of my ability to look like Him. That's why I crave a deeper understanding of true sex and maybe why you do too. *Yada* is spiritual in a *spiritually unique* manner. Philip Yancey wrote,

> If humanity serves as your religion, then sex becomes an act of worship. On the other hand, if God is the object of your religion, then romantic love becomes an unmistakable pointer, a rumor of transcendences as loud as any we hear on earth.[9]

That's why boys like girls.
(And why they like to kiss.)

the lesbian question

everyone's story is different."

That's how Rachel began hers.

"I grew up wishing I was a man."

She went on to share a memory from her early childhood when she wanted to play with blocks. Those big primary-colored blocks printed with a mortar-and-brick pattern. Everyone wanted to play with them, but three boys were monopolizing them. Rachel dared to walk over to join in.

"I don't remember what they said," continued Rachel. "I just know that I wasn't allowed to play. And I believed it was because I was a girl. I decided then that my life would be better if I were a boy."

Rachel grew up in a Christian home. She knew God loved her. She knew He'd made her. She just felt like a boy trapped in a girl's body. She played with boys and had very few friendships with girls. She kept her hair short and didn't mind being mistaken for a boy. As time moved on, she grew into a young adult—and discovered that sex is emotional.

"It was very easy for me to manipulate friendships with women who would become emotionally dependent," admits Rachel. "Women who have never had a same-sex attraction would allow themselves to become physically intimate with me because I fed that emotional attachment so much."

All the while, Rachel made her way through youth group and graduated from a prominent Christian university. No one knew.

"It was my secret," she says. "I felt ignored. I knew God made all things good. But I had these feelings that weren't good. Not how He meant me to be. But then why didn't He help me? Why didn't He change me? I was also afraid to say anything. Afraid that if I ever said anything out loud I would never be able to take it back. And I didn't want this to become my identity."

Silence didn't help. It only made things worse. Rachel spent a lot of lonely years just white-knuckling it to live what she believed was a righteous life. But a few years ago, she mustered up the courage to talk to her pastor's wife about her struggle. Unimaginable freedom soon began to lighten her heart, and she was able to find the help she needed in community.

Things are different now. At age twenty-seven, Rachel is one of two women in recovery whom I asked to help me write this chapter by sharing their stories. The other is approximately sixty years old and has been living in full freedom from same-sex attraction since the 1980s. Though the older woman's story may seem a greater example of victory, Rachel's story—still new in its freedom—intrigued me.

Maybe it's the fact that she's already helping teens find hope for moving beyond same-sex attraction. Maybe it's her newfound comfort with fashion and makeup. Maybe it's the crush she has on a guy, who she's not quite sure is crushing back. Maybe it's the giddy joy in her voice as she candidly shares with me her story of freedom.

I like Rachel.

She's my new friend, and I asked her to pray over me as I write this chapter.

I imagine that if you're questioning your sexual identity, I would enjoy spending time with you just as much as I do with Rachel. And I wish that we could talk about your story. But since we can't, I'd like to give you a few words of encouragement. So let's talk about some things I've learned from Rachel.

Don't Live Under Any Label

Rachel says that when she starts working with a teen who is struggling, she refuses to let her use labels. Don't let the gay/lesbian/bisexual/transsexual movement slap a label on you. And don't let Christians who judge your struggle to be more scandalous than theirs label you as somehow less precious in God's eyes.

The Christian response to homosexuality has been splintered at best. Some preach acceptance and support gay marriage and homosexual clergy. Others picket and press God's law into the faces of the struggling. I've seen both extremes alienate people from searching out the truth of God's heart on the matter. Esteemed Bible teacher Beth Moore wrote,

> One of God's priority purposes for the Church is for her to be a
> welcoming place of restoration and recovery for all who desire
> to be freed from the captivity of sin. Homophobia is the last

thing I'm suggesting for the Church; however, our current unwillingness to admit the problem, embrace the repentant, and aid in biblical restoration—all symptomatic of homophobia—has left us more vulnerable to evil than helpful to the captive.[1]

The first thing I want to say to you if you are struggling with lesbianism is this: I'm so sorry for the way the church has made you feel. Your sin, if you are acting on your temptation, is not a "worse" sin. It is a different sin. And it does not exclude you from your position as a member of the family of Christ. You do not have to decide if you are a Christian or if you are struggling with same-sex attraction. If you embrace Jesus as Savior, you are a Christian and Jesus would welcome you with open arms and risk alienation along with you in order to help you find your way back into truth. He loves you and longs for you to walk in freedom. And I have wonderful news. You can. Just like Rachel.

You are not gay.

You are a daughter of Christ. Struggling with same-sex attraction is a symptom of life lived in a fallen world.

Stop labeling yourself.

Drag Your Struggle into the Light

One thing I'm certain of as you seek answers to this struggle: there are no easy answers. If there were, you would have found them. But I believe that a critical step in everyone's path to freedom is telling someone about whatever it is that binds you. Rachel mentioned Ephesians 5, where the apostle Paul wrote,

Have nothing to do with the fruitless deeds of darkness, but rather *expose them*. For it is shameful even to mention what the disobedient do in secret. But everything exposed by the light becomes visible, for it is light that makes everything visible. This is why it is said: "Wake up, O sleeper, rise from the dead, and Christ will shine on you."

—EPHESIANS 5:11-14

It's not easy to bring your secrets out into the light by talking to people who are safe. Oddly enough, it can be even more difficult to confess your temptation when you haven't acted on it; something inside of you says you don't have to confess because you haven't sinned. But the need is no less great if you've been silently struggling alone in your fantasies; this is the point at which you can win the battle with fewer scars because you have not yet acted on your temptations.

While I can promise that there is freedom in confession, I can't promise it'll be comfortable at first. Have you ever been watching a movie in the dark when someone burst into the room and turned on the light? It hurts your eyes. It's not comfortable. Confessing your struggles to someone else will be a lot like that. A bit of a shock to your system. A little uncomfortable. But having taken this step with my own secrets, I know that it's not nearly as horrible as it seems it will be.

Drag it into the light.

Identify the Lies

I have learned something about same-sex attraction that may ruffle some Christian feathers: it was not your decision to struggle with it, if you do. Or your friend's, if she does. A girl doesn't wake up one day and decide she'll be attracted to the next girl who walks through the door. No, that's not how it works. While it is your choice whether to act on those desires or to comply with God's standards of sexuality, it was not your decision to enlist in the internal war.

Somewhere along the way, something took root in you that grew into this struggle. Sexuality is undeniably complex. Biological, cul-

the Progression of a lie

In *Lies Young Women Believe*, Nancy Leigh DeMoss and I wrote about the stages to believing a lie. Maybe knowing this will help you identify where you started to believe one about your sexuality.

1. **We listen to a lie.** We frequently get close to messages that are contrary to God's truth.

2. **We dwell on a lie.** We converse about those lies and consider deeply and regularly what is said without dwelling on truth or asking the advice of others who know God's truth.

3. **We believe a lie.** We believe that the lie is more trustworthy than what God says in His Word.

4. **We act on a lie.** We sin.[2]

tural, social, and spiritual factors converge to create a perceived identity that may or may not be in alignment with God's chosen plan for your life. How do you ever figure it all out to get to the deep roots of confusion?

My friend Lynn Nold was the person Rachel chose to talk to about her struggle. For years, Lynn has been praying for people with addictions, depression, and seemingly insurmountable spiritual struggles. And I have watched these individuals walk into new freedom through her counsel and prayers offered in faith. Her ministry is effective because she has learned the power of uprooting lies. You see, the patterns, behaviors, and addictions we struggle with are often the fruit of a lie that took root years ago.

For Rachel it was the lie that her life would be better if she were a man. To uproot that lie, she began to feast on scriptures that revealed how good it is to be a girl. I hope that you, too, no matter your struggles in life, take time to see what God's Word really says about being a woman, because it's so often not well represented in our contemporary culture, including our churches. The Bible affirms women in a way that was radically unique considering the highly male-dominated time in which it was written. I often meditate on how very much God must love me as a woman to be so bold in what was recorded in Scripture. Let me quickly show you what I mean.

The Old Testament affirms women as equal partners with men. Genesis 1:27 says that men and women *together* mirror the image of God. (We've covered that one, right?) The next verse challenges both men and women to be co-regents of the world *together*. Women are never instructed in Scripture to passively sit on the sidelines. They are a vital part of God's plan to rule, subdue, and manage the earth. (If they can do that, then a little girl can surely build with those big cardboard building blocks!)

In the New Testament, we find even more affirmation. It presented a startling contrast to every literary tradition of the day for God to inspire the writer of Matthew to include women in the lineage of Jesus Christ. This was a bold statement in a patriarchal, misogynistic culture. Most astonishing, Jesus Himself chose *a woman* to be the first to testify of His resurrection. It was Mary, according to Matthew 28:1–10, who was charged to go tell the men that He'd risen. This flew in the face of Pharisaic law, which said a woman's testimony was not admissible in a tribunal. Back in the day of Jesus, the value of women was terribly misunderstood, even as it is today. But my heart is encouraged that He, in written and living word, pushed against cultural untruth.

Rachel began her own search for scriptures that affirm her womanhood. And here's how she feels about being a girl today:

> The truth for me is that I am female and there is good in my femininity. I believe that my gifts of teaching and counseling are more powerfully and beautifully expressed in the context of my true sexuality.

We're rarely able to identify lies on our own. By its very nature, a lie is deceptive. Rachel needed Lynn's help to discover the truth. You need help too. A few years ago, I wrote a book with Nancy Leigh DeMoss called *Lies Young Women Believe*. It would be a great tool to learn more about identifying lies and learning to walk in truth concerning your sexuality.

Find a Place of Grace-Filled Truth
That Encourages You to Look Like God

We're all somewhat broken.

That makes the church somewhat broken, and it might be one reason why finding a safe place has been so difficult for you. Please know that I understand that loneliness, though the kind of sin I struggled with was different (not better or worse, just different). For ten years, I carried my secret of having had sex with a guy who is now a complete stranger to me. I know what loneliness feels like.

I also know how good it feels to walk with a local church body that knows all my sins and loves me still. Rachel is finding that too. And I can hear the freedom in her voice.

Lynn was able to help Rachel find freedom because she was both understanding (she didn't stuff God's rules about sex in Rachel's face) and truthful (she didn't tell Rachel that her choices don't matter to God). It is my prayer that you'd be able to find a place of grace-filled truth that helps you want to look like God.

What do I mean by that?

I believe that Paul's three most powerful responses to the misuse of sexuality are found in 1 Corinthians 6:12–20; Ephesians 5:31–32; and Romans 1:21–27. In each of these—relevant to me, as one who had sex outside of marriage; relevant to my husband, who has struggled with porn; and relevant to you no matter the details of your sexual struggle—Paul anchored his response in a look back at Genesis. Conspicuously absent from each of these passages is any appeal to God's law or rules about sex. (Equally important, he also did not rationalize sinful behavior with cheap grace.) Instead, he reminded us what our sexuality represents:

> Although they claimed to be wise, they became fools and
> exchanged the glory of the immortal God for images made
> to look like mortal man and birds and animals and reptiles.
> (Romans 1:22–23)

In other words, he reminded us that we were created to glorify God. That we are statues of God. We are—as distinct male and female individuals—His image, made not of stone but of flesh. In a blissful marriage union of one man and one woman, we look a lot like Him.

You see, if we follow God's design for *yada,* we celebrate the beautiful diversity of maleness and femaleness. But today we've exchanged that image for something that looks a whole lot more animalistic than divine. The Kate Hudson–ish worldview of sex so common today doesn't point to God, but to animals. Paul continued on, just in case we aren't getting it:

> Therefore God gave them over in the sinful desires of their
> hearts to sexual impurity for the degrading of their bodies
> with one another. They exchanged the truth of God for a
> lie.… Because of this, God gave them over to shameful lusts.

Even their women exchanged natural relations for unnatural ones. In the same way the men also abandoned natural relations with women and were inflamed with lust for one another. Men committed indecent acts with other men. (verses 24–27)

God's design in creating you female and calling you to a life of purity, which may or may not include a one-man/one-woman relationship, is meant to point to Him. In light of His purpose in creating us distinctly male and female, God's guidelines concerning your sexuality—and mine—are not arbitrary.

Here's the deal: homosexual sex is sin, just as my heterosexual sex outside of marriage at age fifteen was sin. And our stories, though they may be unique in certain ways, are a little bit the same.

Maybe Rachel is right. Maybe our stories are all different.

But I think in some ways they are all very much the same.

9

sex is not a solo sport

in the late 1940s and early 1950s, a guy named Alfred Kinsey (known today as the father of sexology), released groundbreaking research on sex. His focus group–based research drastically changed cultural perspectives on sex. Sadly, his work is respected even though he often relied on prisoners and prostitutes for his research because average people were reluctant to talk about sex. Obviously, this flawed approach made his findings unreliable.

One of the subjects Kinsey opened for debate was that of masturbation. Maybe you've heard the joke that grew out of his research: 98 percent of people masturbate and the other 2 percent are lying.

Is that true?

You want to know.

A lot of young women are wondering.

Probably because a lot of young women are struggling. Maybe even you.

In one women's magazine, 65 percent of eighteen- to twenty-five-year-olds admitted to masturbating while looking at porn online.[1] In the same magazine, a reader commented, "When I was younger, I turned to the Internet to read up on this masturbation thing I'd been hearing about. It was enlightening, and I'm thankful I had those online resources in the privacy of my bedroom."[2]

When I was speaking at a Christian college, the dean of women told me that a substantial number of women on the campus were doing the same thing. How did she know? They were sharing links with each other...and tips. (Embarrassingly for them, the school was tracking their online conversations!)

But not everyone is talking about this subject so openly. This morning, on my way to my parents' mountain house to write, I stopped by the office. My assistant, Eileen, slipped into my hand a long letter sent to me by a reader. Strong Christian girl. Freshman at a Christian college. Crazy about a junior at the same college. Got her first kiss this summer at the age of eighteen, from her first boyfriend. But she's not feeling it. The purity, I mean.

> All of that being said, I am not sexually pure.... I have been held under the lie of masturbation.... And just when I think I've kicked the habit for good, one lonely sleepless night steals it away again.... Dannah, you're the first person on earth besides me who knows. I haven't told a single soul. I don't know if I could. The shame it would bring.... I don't know if I could utter those words aloud to another human being.

The letter kinda ripped a hole in my heart...and my outline. I've counseled all too many teen- and college-aged girls about this. It's a common struggle. Too common for her to feel so stinkin' lonely.

Lately, it's one of the most frequent topics in letters I receive from girls pleading for clarity. One high school senior literally collapsed into my arms and nearly fainted when she finally got the words out. That kind of isolation isn't going to help anyone. So let me be honest with you.

I never, ever struggled with masturbation when I was in high school or college. So it has been difficult at times for me to counsel lonely hearts. I've worked with women who are well into their middle-aged years or beyond and, like me, have never struggled. Masturbation is not every woman's struggle the way it is every man's.

Things got a little more complicated—or maybe less so—about eight years ago. I experienced a deep and fairly public rejection. The details of that aren't secret but also aren't relevant. During this time I began to experience dark and sexually oppressive dreams from which I'd awaken sexually aroused and tempted to masturbate.[3]

I think I understand your loneliness now.

And I have a better sense of how to answer you.

First of all, is it sin? Well, the bad news is that the Bible offers no direct teaching on masturbation.[4] Does that mean we don't have any information in Scripture to direct our behavior when we feel tempted? Not at all. We can look at other principles to answer our question.

Let's begin with a definition of *sin*. The Hebrew language of the Bible sometimes uses an archery term for sin. Here's an example:

> For I acknowledge my transgressions, and my sin [*chatta*] is always before me.
>
> —PSALM 51:3, NKJV

In that verse, David was lamenting his failure before God by committing adultery with Bathsheba and then murdering her husband to hide it. Both sins—adultery and murder—warranted a word that described the sin as something other than God's intent and design. Let me show you what I mean.

The word *chatta* means "to miss the mark." In other words, sin is missing God's intended purpose for our lives—His bull's-eye, if you will.

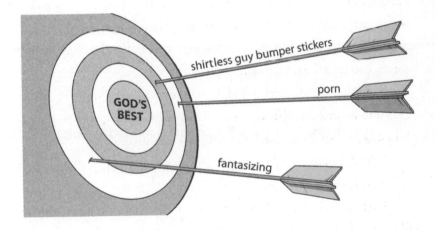

Sexually speaking, our bull's-eye, or "mark," is *yada*. Our goal is to know, to be known, and to be deeply respected. Now, from that basis, let's consider the question of whether masturbation is a sin.

It's a Sin If It Distorts God's Design

Christ blows the ill-fitting door off any defense we might present for entertaining sexual thoughts about a man who is not our husband. In Matthew 5:27–28, He said, "You have heard that it was said, 'Do not commit adultery.' But I tell you that anyone who looks at a woman lustfully has already committed adultery with her in his heart."

Obviously, if it is sinful for a man to lust after a woman, it is also sinful for us to lust after a guy. (You might consider that verse if you have pictures of shirtless, buff-bodied guys posted as bumper stickers on your Facebook page.) If your eyes and mind are engaged in pornography or mental fantasy involving a guy when you are masturbating, you are sinning.

Why?

Because you cannot know, be known by, or be respected by a picture in a magazine or on the Internet. That's one way porn so utterly twists God's intended design for sex.

It's a Sin If It Has Become an Addiction

If you are controlled by or enslaved to anything other than God, it is a sin. The apostle Paul wrote,

> "Everything is permissible for me"—but I will not be mastered by anything.
>
> —1 CORINTHIANS 6:12

The church in Corinth had been misinterpreting a teaching about everything being permissible. They had excused certain sins by saying that Christ had taken away all sin, and so they were free to live as they pleased. That's not entirely true. Paul explained that some behaviors that are not specifically sinful in themselves still are not appropriate for a follower of Christ because they can lead us away from God and His intentions for our sexuality.

If you cannot fall asleep at night without the ritual of masturbating, or if you find yourself planning your life so you can be alone to masturbate, it has become an addictive behavior—and that means it's sin.

Aiming for God's Ideal

But even those clear answers still leave a gray area over which many scholarly Christian psychologists and theologians have debated for years. What if you occasionally masturbate in a quick moment—and I do mean moment—with no thought of lust and without any harm to your body? Is *that* okay?

Corn flakes won't help!

The strangest fact I discovered as I did my research for this chapter: Kellogg's Corn Flakes apparently were created in the early 1900s to cure young men of their masturbatory desires. Dr. John Harvey Kellogg, director of the Battle Creek Sanitarium, advocated eating his breakfast cereal as part of a healthy and bland diet, which he believed would curb the desire to self-gratify!

Guess what? They don't work![5]

Let me first say that I don't think you should beat yourself up over it or consider it a "sick, vile, filthy, and disgusting" secret that "drives a wedge between God" and you. (Those are the words of my friend who wrote me today. Maybe they describe your feelings as well.) The great depth of shame concerning masturbation versus the lack of shame for outright sexual intercourse amazes me. When a girl comes to me for counseling concerning masturbation, she often is not capable of uttering the words. There's something unique about the heart's response to this act.

Though our feelings don't determine whether it's right or wrong, one thing I am sure of: the response isn't rational. Masturbation is a nearly universal act for guys and a common one for girls. There is no need to bury yourself under a heap of shame. You will survive this and so will your relationship with God.

> If a believer realizes that the Holy Spirit is leading him into self-rule, he will not fall into passivity; on the contrary, he will advance greatly in his spiritual life. "The fruit of the Spirit is... temperance" (Galatians 5:22–23, KJV).
>
> —Watchman Nee[6]

So why do so many people feel so bad about it? I think discomfort with masturbation is an inbuilt check and balance to protect the purpose of the marriage bed. What is that purpose? To bring us into intimate communion. *Yada* is a picture of a *relationship* with God. It can be experienced only in the context of a male/female *relationship*. Solo sex may bring some sense of pleasure or release, but ultimately it falls short of truly satisfying our built-in desire for *yada* because it doesn't lead us to know or be known; it doesn't accurately reflect the image of God the way the union of two souls is meant to do.

While many girls seem to experience deep guilt over masturbation, the media and culture seem to treat it as a matter-of-fact behavior, as unquestioned as other solo activities like playing solitaire or reading a book. It's not like that at all. Sex is not a solo sport.

The authors of the aptly titled book *Authentic Human Sexuality* describe sexual desire in the context of a drive to community:

> Deeply embedded within each one of us is a divine longing for wholeness that sends us reaching beyond ourselves to God and others. Sexual desire helps us recognize our incompleteness as human beings and causes us to seek the other to find a fuller meaning in life.... Authentic sexuality urges us toward a rich sharing of our lives.[7]

By contrast, masturbation is an individual and lonely act that robs us of the dependent and communal nature that sex was designed to have. As Lauren Winner has observed, "To return sex to its proper place within creation, to revivify a gracious and salutary sexual existence, we need to root out modern and hyperindividualistic notions about sex, and come to understand the place of sex in the Christian— and human—community."[8]

It is this fundamental call to community or relationship, and the sacred, perhaps sacramental, approach to sexuality, that calls me to view masturbation as missing the mark of God's purpose for my sexual desire. My sexual desire is meant to draw me to my husband, and any act that does otherwise abuses and misuses that desire. According to the definition of the Greek and Hebrew words for sin used in the Bible, masturbation is a sin. The very idea of "self-pleasuring" goes against the *yada* ideal of knowing another intimately.

What does that mean in practical terms for you, a single girl waiting for Mr. Right? I think it's critically important to view your sexual desire as a calling for your future husband and to avoid developing habits that will rob you of your ability to allow *him* to bring pleasure to you. Remember that habitual masturbation could train your body to be hyperresponsive to self and make it difficult to respond to your husband's stimulation. Self-pleasure—while it cannot be viewed as an unforgivable spiritual failure—must be viewed as a hyperindividualistic response to a desire meant to be fulfilled in marital communion.

Be careful to do everything you can to avoid falling into masturbation. If you do find yourself struggling, tell an older godly woman.

But don't be surprised if you experience some temptation. We are, after all, sexual beings. Many women awaken sexually aroused and sometimes even having a spontaneous orgasm. This is called nocturnal orgasm. It's natural and may be a part of God's design to release sexual tension, much like a wet dream for guys. Don't condemn yourself for experiencing temptation. It is not sin unless you yield to it. I can personally tell you that it is possible to experience the temptation without giving in to the sin of masturbation.

While self-pleasuring is certainly not grounds for groveling in shame, it's also not something to casually accept as a way to meet your sexual longings. Always, the real question is, "Does this lead me closer to or further from God's divine design for me to know, to be known, and to be deeply respected?"

I'm sure of this: sex is not a solo sport.

10

our porn problem

i was nineteen years old, and we'd been dating for a little over a year.

Bob Gresh broke one of our cardinal dating rules that night: he took me to the basement of my parents' house, and we sat alone in the dark together. We never sat alone in the dark. We had a rule about "staying public."

Clearly this was serious.

There, on the mud-colored shag carpet, he revealed to me the darkest secret of his heart. For the past few years, he'd been tormented by porn and its power over him. It was easy to read between the lines. He wasn't asking me for help. He was giving me an "out."

"Do you really want to be in a relationship with a guy like *me*?" he was asking.

I cried. Kissed him on the cheek. Prayed with him and went to bed a little numb.

It will go away when we're married, I thought.

He was thinking the same thing in the room next to my parents' as he drifted off to sleep that night.

It didn't go away when we were married.

What if your boyfriend is struggling with porn?

Now there's a question that's tough for me to answer. The fact that Bob has fought a hard battle to overcome it sometimes makes me afraid that I may be biased in how I answer your fears. (How's that for transparency?) I often find myself torn between Christian women who have a zero-tolerance policy for porn and treat men who struggle with it like future child abusers and those who have an overly tolerant approach that leaves no room for God's truth to rescue the addict (often these women are struggling themselves).

While Bob and I have found a place of biblical truth to deal with our porn problem, it seems that many in the church still have not even begun to operate in truth, and that makes it complicated. I just can't answer this one alone.

So I asked for some help. I e-mailed five of the men I most respect (other than my husband, whom I am dearly in love with and whom I deeply respect): my pastor, my husband's best friend, a co-worker, a favorite male author, and a pastor who traveled with me on a group missions trip. These are men whose walk with the Lord is filled with integrity and truth. I trust them because I see Jesus in them. So the answers that follow are straight from the heart of men.

Before we get to the answer of what to do if your boyfriend is struggling with porn, we should cover a few basic facts.

Porn Is Ubiquitous

Pastor Bryan Spang wrote to me: "The struggle with porn is a very ubiquitous problem among men." *Ubiquitous.* Merriam-Webster.com defines it as "existing or being everywhere; constantly encountered."

Chances are, your boyfriend *is* struggling with pornography, even if he hasn't told you about it. According to *Christianity Today,* 70 percent of American men ages eighteen to thirty-four admit to viewing porn once a month. (And it's not just a guy's problem. One out of every three visitors to online porn sites is a woman.)[1] Frankly, I think those stats are a little low. That's the number of guys "admitting" to it and who are viewing it "once a month." What about the guys who don't admit it? What about the ones who only view it every other month? Or once a year? As my husband facilitates our live events, he's finding it harder and harder to locate a male mentor to share a testimony of living porn-free his entire life. Such men are rare these days.

Nate Larkin, author and founder of the Samson Society, put it this way when he wrote to me: "Not all guys use porn, but all guys have seen porn and all guys like it." I had to sit with that for a while.

All guys like it?

Then it occurred to me that Eve was naked when she met Adam. And he liked it. I don't know that for certain, but it seems like God was making a pretty bold statement when He inspired the writer of Genesis to pen this line: "The man and his wife were both naked, and they felt no shame" (2:25).

Nate went on to explain the ubiquity of porn and why—at a first glance, anyway—all guys like it or are drawn to it. He said, "It stimulates a God-given instinct. It takes a beautiful urge in the wrong direction, promising a shortcut to sexual intimacy while actually leading to depersonalization and depravity. That's what makes it so alluring and so dangerous."

you are not alone

Porn is not just a guy's problem. One of every six women in the United States is struggling at some level. Are you one of them? You're not alone, and you don't have to fight this battle on your own either. In fact, you shouldn't or you probably won't win. As I shared in this chapter, I've rarely seen the porn battle won outside of authentic community. Dirty Girls Ministries founder Crystal Renaud fought the battle of porn and celebrated five years of victory before I met her at a conference where she shared her story. We both have a passion for breaking through the shame of loneliness. She says, "It's my hope that every woman who struggles with porn, thinking she's alone, would discover that she's not." So, if you're tired of feeling like you're all alone, log on to www.crystalrenaud.com today and get serious about winning the fight![2]

Porn Is Dangerous

Porn does damage to people and to relationships. Even the secular world recognizes its danger. That's why actor David Duchovny checked into rehab when his online porn addiction got out of control. That's why the marriage of supermodel Christie Brinkley and Peter Cook couldn't survive his three-thousand-dollar-a-month porn habit, which may or may not have contributed to his cheating on her. That's why porn star Jenna Jameson cried on *Oprah* when she thought about her little boys knowing what she's done.

Porn is dangerous.

It ravages hearts and lives. It creates a never-satisfied thirst in men and women who use it. Hear me on this: porn lures its victims away from *yada*. It drags a man—or a woman—into isolation, severing the ability to know and be known. You cannot know pixels on a screen or ink on a page.

The illusory promise of porn is that it will satisfy that deep need for intimacy. It doesn't. But it succeeds in convincing the user that just one more day...one more look...will be enough.

You remember dopamine? The chemical that washes over your brain when you have sex? smoke a cigarette? work out? do anything that offers pleasure? Remember, dopamine is value-neutral. It doesn't distinguish "good" pleasure from "bad" pleasure. There's lots of dopamine overload in porn users. And that creates addiction. Just one more look is never enough. So the user is pulled deeper and deeper into the vortex of a huge worldwide industry that cares nothing about relationships but very much about money. It has no regard for the destruction porn leaves in its path.

Even when there is not obvious relational destruction, there is often a sense of "something wrong" in marriages where porn is a factor. My husband wrote a book for teen guys about this, and in it he noted,

> When marriage comes along and everything doesn't happen just like in our fantasies, we find ourselves frustrated and unfulfilled by what should be fantastic and fun. We can't find the satisfaction that God meant for us to know. We've robbed our own marriage bed.[3]

Many men have admitted to using porn prior to marriage and then finding the marriage bed unfulfilling. One man said, "Our wedding night was a big disappointment. I'd brought the only sexual experience I knew into a loving relationship, and there was no connection.... I was crushed with the realization that my wife wasn't exciting."[4]

Think about it. Peter Cook couldn't find satisfaction with three-time *Sports Illustrated* Swimsuit Edition cover model Christie Brinkley! She wasn't enough, even though she's lauded universally as one of the most beautiful women alive. Even in her fifties, she's stunning.

A man can have the most beautiful wife alive and still struggle with porn. No matter what excuses a guy may give, his use of porn is *not* about you and is *not* your fault for not being beautiful enough.

Porn Won't Go Away When You Get Married

My husband was a virgin on our wedding night. He fought for that. He wanted to stand pure before God. But mentally he was not a virgin.

He knew that, and he hated it. But he reasoned that once he started having sex, certainly the lust would stop. It didn't.

A lot of guys believe that their porn problem will go away once they're married. Their girlfriends believe the same thing. It's one of the most frequently asked questions at our ministry events. Sometimes it's a teary-eyed fiancée asking if marriage will cure her soon-to-be husband. Other times it's a fifteen-year-old missionary kid, desperately hoping that his hellish roller coaster of failing and succeeding will end in a few years when he's married. But the lure of porn is never quenched by marital sex because porn has almost nothing to do with real love and real sex. It's as counterfeit as a counterfeit can be. Making something holy, wicked. Something loving, aggressive. Something intimate, unaccountable. Porn satisfies lust, not love.

Nate Larkin told me, "Porn corrodes a marriage because lust kills love. Love gives; lust takes. Love sees a person; lust sees a body. Love is about you; lust is about me and my own gratification."

Love seeks…knows…respects.

Lust couldn't care less.

Back to the brain. (It always goes there for me. Sex really doesn't happen in the lower part of our bodies. It happens between our ears.) The area of the brain that experiences lust is the hypothalamus—not to be confused with the nearby thalamus, located in the deep limbic system, which aids us in bonding and true love. When a man feeds the deep limbic system's love mechanism with healthy doses of love chemicals, the love controls the lust and uses physical desire to enhance a marriage. When a man continually feeds the hypothalamus with porn, the lust takes control. It stamps out his ability to love and to experience *yada*.

And that can make it so that even if he's in the same room with you, he's not really there. His brain is fried on porn.

Porn Makes It Hard to Respect a Man

You alone can never beat porn. You won't be enough. Marriage is not your boyfriend's coming savior. Only Jesus can be that. And his Savior calls out to him, "Be holy, because I am holy" (1 Peter 1:16). The guy who is pursuing holiness is worthy of your respect.

I have the privilege of having a husband who hates what porn does to his relationship with God and me, so he fights it. And he's winning. The tremendous intimacy we experience in his victory reminds me how vacuous our love was when he was in the grip of the Enemy. Saying no to porn enables both of our hearts to say yes to each other. We miss each other all day long and can't wait to see each other at the end of the day. We want to go to bed together. We wake up touching and talking. I trust him and want his insight into everything that concerns me because I respect him and his opinion more than that of anyone else in the whole world.

But when he was losing the battle, our hearts were numb. We avoided each other and used busyness to dull our senses. I dreaded days when we had a lot of time together. I tried to be asleep before he came to bed and put a pillow between me and his side of the bed so we wouldn't have to touch. I could not have cared less about his opinions.

It's hard to respect a man who uses porn. Since *yada* mandates an atmosphere of respect, you can't have it and porn too!

Wake up, church! We can't just accept porn as the norm. Even though it may be the norm, it's not okay. Doesn't the word *normal* equal big, fat, and average? When I take a test, I don't want to be at the top of the bell curve. I want to be at the extreme drop of that curve that represents the highest scoring 5 percent of test takers. Sexually speaking, porn may be the top of the bell curve, but it's not where Bob and I want to live.

Porn users aren't always having the best sex, and they definitely aren't experiencing the best marriages. This was so eloquently written about by liberal feminist author Naomi Wolf in an article for *New York* magazine. Though her sexual values may be antithetical to mine in many ways, she recognized a great danger of porn when she observed, "In the end porn doesn't whet men's appetites—it turns them off the real thing.... The onslaught of porn is responsible for deadening male libido in relation to real women, and leading men to see fewer and fewer women as 'porn-worthy.'" Wolf advocated boycotting porn, not because it is morally bad in her eyes, but because "greater supply of the stimulant equals diminished capacity."[5]

So Should You Dump Him?

I think there is another question hiding in the hearts of the college-aged women who ask, "What if my boyfriend is using porn?" I think, at the heart of it, they want the answer to this: "Should I dump him?"

Maybe.

Maybe not.

lady Gaga, victoria's Secret, and the girl next door

Are you a Lady Gaga video fanatic? Do you spend all your extra cash at Victoria's Secret? Does *The Girls Next Door* on *E!* intrigue you?

Can you say, "Porn has gone mainstream"?

Porn stars like Holly Madison and Jenna Jameson are now considered mainstream celebrities. The clothing worn and sexual acts portrayed in videos created by the likes of Lady Gaga (yes, she writes catchy songs!) and Christina Aguilera are undeniably pornographic, but many who watch them are numb to how inappropriate they are. Especially troublesome is the violent nature of the sexual portrayals, complete with diamond-studded handcuffs and bras with semiautomatic weapons sewn into them, which is so antithetical to the loving purpose of sex that God intended.

And though this may step on your toes, passive acts like spending money at Victoria's Secret or Abercrombie & Fitch, both of which have normalized soft porn with their commercials, catalogs, and fashion shows, only creates growth in an insidious industry, not to mention the way the nudity and sensuality portrayed numbs you to the beauty of *yada*. Could it be that you are—without knowing it—contributing to our porn problem in the church?

I've counseled unmarried women in both directions. There are a great number of factors to consider when your boyfriend is looking at porn. Now that you know how high the stakes are, let's touch on them quickly and trust that God will guide you with the details.

Did He Admit the Struggle?

All the men I asked said that if a guy admits his struggle, he is likely not willing to be overcome by the porn. He wants to fight it. The key is humble admission and repentance. "A guy who is honest and vulnerable about his temptation with porn, even if his fight against it is not 100 percent successful, can make a great life partner," said Nate Larkin.

On the other hand, if he's getting caught, lies by saying that he doesn't "really like porn," or claims that *he* "can overcome it"—or if he is brazen about it and says porn's okay—he's not safe. As an unmarried couple, you have no obligation to him. You do have an obligation to yourself and to God to aim for a higher, purer relationship that can more genuinely reflect the image God has in mind for sex. You are called to seek a love that is a picture of God's passionate love for us.

Is He Willing to Talk to Other Godly Men About It?

Very few guys overcome their porn problem in isolation, but I've seen great victory when they walk in community with other men. (Let me say that I believe the most important factor is the indwelling of the Holy Spirit, but I also believe that Scripture teaches us to walk in community to overcome sin.)

My husband attends one of Nate Larkin's Samson Society meetings every Monday night. These men talk about real things in real time and hold each other accountable to pursue lives of holiness. This is one of my husband's tethers to God: other men holding his feet to the fire of holiness.

If your boyfriend or fiancé is willing to talk to other men and find community, he is probably a guy worth sticking with. On the other hand, if he is too prideful to tell another person about his struggle or if he jumps in for short periods of accountability and then jumps out because he considers himself quickly "cured," I advise one thing: run!

> God resists the proud, but gives grace to the humble.
>
> —1 PETER 5:5, NKJV

A man who is too proud to confess his faults is going to face some difficult times in the future. You might not want to be a part of that.

I know you have more concerns than those two questions can address, so I'd suggest that you seek out community too. Find someone to talk with not just about your boyfriend's struggles but yours as well. Make sure another wise, godly person is offering guidance into what may be the most critical decision of your life: whom you will marry.

One more question while we are on the subject: are you walking in holiness in this area? More and more, I hear from women caught up in the grip of porn. If this is you, I believe that you will face destruction and a devastating lack of intimacy if you don't admit your powerlessness and start walking out victory in community.

Tell someone today if you or your boyfriend is struggling.

exclusive love

i tried to buy body chocolate today.

It was a first for me.

Tonight I'm going to a bridal shower for my intern, Cali Galloway, and I wanted to give her something memorable. So I went to Chocolate Madness, where I remembered seeing it before, but I couldn't find it. I guess they were out. The only people in the store were me and the middle-aged chocolate-selling man, decked out in a white apron and blue latex gloves. Seemed totally inappropriate to start up a conversation about body chocolate with him. When he asked what I was looking for, I fumbled for a moment and then clumsily pointed to the nearest thing in the display case. Ended up buying a little box of cool-looking raspberry thingies that cost way too much and have a name I can't pronounce.

Then I went down the street to a shop where I bought Cali some lingerie instead.

It is my absolute delight to share in the preparation of this sweet virgin bride for her honeymoon. Our whole office is giddy with excitement for her. After all, we don't live, breathe, preach, and teach purity for any reason other than a full and unashamed celebration of sexual oneness between a bride and her groom.

Purity is *not* about *not* having sex. It's about waiting to have it right.

Here at Pure Freedom, my staff and I love sex.

And we celebrate it.

So did the Jewish culture! Their celebration of the sexual union began with the preparation of the bride and groom. A bit more formal than our bridal showers, but really cool. Let me explain.

It started with a visit from his father to her father. Some sort of payment had to be made for this bride. If the groom could provide an acceptable bride price, the marriage *ketubah* (a contract of agreed-upon standards of behavior and care) was written up, and the young couple was officially betrothed or engaged. The groom then went off to prepare a place for them to live. Sometimes he'd build an entirely

here comes the bride

Still waiting for a guy to pop the question? No worries. It might not be time yet. Check out the average age of a bride in the following countries![1]

England	—	32
Jamaica	—	31
Canada	—	31
China	—	30
U.S.	—	25
India	—	19

new home, but often he built a room onto his father's house. When the building was completed, the groom wasted no time in retrieving his bride. He'd gather all his friends, and they'd sing and dance and bang pots and pans in the streets on their way to claim his girl. Then he would carry her through the streets, shouting and rejoicing that he was ready and could provide for her.

The Jewish tradition was to cover the bride and groom with a *chuppah* (pronounced hoo-pah) as they walked through the streets. It was a big banner or canopy that covered only them, signifying the *exclusiveness* of their intimacy. Though the entire community was involved in the celebration of their union, the *chuppah* was symbolic of their relationship being separated...holy. Only the two of them could be under the *chuppah*.

And make no mistake about where this entourage was headed. They were marching the blushing bride and groom straight to their marriage bed. (Yep. That's right. The sex happened before the big wedding feast.) Shameless in its sexual expression was the Jewish tradition of giving the bride and groom white bed linens for their consummation. They would bring them out the next day with blood evidence (from the stretching or breaking of the woman's hymen) that the two now were physically one (*echad*). In the Jewish culture, the shed blood served as a deeply meaningful allusion to every other high and holy covenant they'd ever taken part in.

God's Love Language

We've already seen that the book of Genesis—and our very design as humans, distinctly male and female—reveals marriage as a picture of

God and His *relational* love. As our study of the word *yada* moves into the New Testament, the curtain opens wider and we can begin to see the *exclusive* nature of God's love.

Exclusive generally means "not with other things or not including others." The love God has for humanity is exclusive. How? Well, in the Old Testament He commands humankind to have "no other gods before Me" (Exodus 20:3, NKJV). In other words, we are to give nothing and no one priority over our relationship with Him. Our love for the One True God cannot be contaminated by other idols.

ebbing the ache

I remember being a junior in college and being single (my guy and I were "taking a break"). It seemed to me like every girl on the planet got a ring during that season of loneliness. No way around it: waiting hurts! You can lean into the pain in a bad way, focusing on your loneliness. Or you can lean into it in a good way, focusing on your love relationship with God. I chose to do the second one and even had a motto:

Jesus Is Enough
God Is Sovereign

It was my goal not to get married until I actually believed that. You know when I knew I believed it? When I started genuinely celebrating after hearing the details of yet another romantic proposal!

Politically incorrect though it may seem, the jealousy of God—designed to protect His creation from false gods intent on the destruction of humankind—demands our exclusive faithfulness. I believe that in the next few paragraphs I can show you that this exclusivity of God's love is meant to be mirrored in the marriage covenant.

Now, while you and I are skipping from Genesis to the New Testament, God carefully left His mark of exclusive love on many pages in between. Just look at all the hints of it in the pages we've skipped.

◎ In Exodus, God called Israel His "treasured possession" (19:5). *Treasured possession* was how a Jewish groom might have referred to his bride. It was a term of endearment.

the Gift of Marriage

One recent issue of *Glamour* magazine dubbed single women who prefer freedom over family as "freemales." Cameron Diaz was touted as a role model for all women. She was quoted, "I love being by myself and I'm really good at it."[2]

Now, the church would never *say* that we've bought into a feminist perspective, but our lives tell a different story. In 1987, 80 percent of Christians felt that the roles of being a wife and a mom were valuable and important to teach to young women. In 2007, only 52 percent felt this way, with 47 percent stating that the roles of marriage and motherhood should *not* be emphasized to young women today. Christian women may not have burned their bras in the 1960s, but

- Psalm 45 is an Old Testament wedding song written about a king and his virgin bride. Its lyrics celebrate a Groom King who could not possibly be human. His throne would "last for ever and ever" (verse 6). Many Bible scholars say it's a prophecy about Christ and the church and the exclusivity of their love.
- In Isaiah 54:5, as the prophet calls the people of Israel back from the sin of loving many gods, he pens it in black and white for all eternity: "For your Maker is your husband."

I could go on pointing to examples of God's deep love as described in many verses between Genesis and the New Testament. The Holy

---

something much more precious and symbolic was burned up within us during the feminist movement: the desire to be wives and moms.

God says, "Marriage is honorable among all, and the bed undefiled" (Hebrews 13:4, NKJV). I believe that God created woman to be in fellowship with man, primarily through marriage. Yes, the apostle Paul was right in saying that it is *good* not to marry so that you can be free to serve God. But *God* said it is *best* to be in an honorable one-man/one-woman marriage. Genesis 2:18 reads, "The LORD God said, 'It is not good for the man to be alone. I will make a helper suitable for him.'"

Want to pursue God's best? Open your heart to the gift of marriage, and let Him make the call.

Spirit inspired writers to pen glimpses of His love all along the way. But glimpses are all that's humanly possible to get because this is a love like none other you've ever known. Pleasure and meaning so out of this world and beyond our capacity to understand that God describes it for us in terms of something earthly—romance that leads to an exclusive commitment.

While the Old Testament hints at marriage as a portrait of our relationship with God, it is not until the writing of the New Testament that we fully understand the picture God had been setting up. Jesus didn't hesitate to point to marriage as a picture of His exclusive love for the church. His language was full of wedding talk. For example, when asked why He and His disciples never fasted, He said, "How can the guests of the bridegroom mourn while he is with them? The time will come when the bridegroom will be taken from them; then they will fast" (Matthew 9:15).

I don't think Jesus just came up with this idea of marriage being a picture of His love. It had been simmering among the Godhead forever and a day. In the writings of the apostles Paul and John, we find rich imagery and symbolism applied to Christ as a groom and to those who have trusted Him as their Savior—or the church—as the bride. These references unveil the purpose of the picture. And here is where it starts to get exclusive.

Let me show you just how beautiful the imagery was to the Jewish girl about your age. Remember those bloody sheets she would bring out on the morning of her wedding feast? The ones she *displayed* the day after her marriage union with her groom was consummated in sexual union? You see, a covenant always was sealed in blood. This symbolism pointed toward the great day when the covenant of Jesus was sealed on the cross in blood.

In fact, do you recognize anything else in the ancient Jewish wedding traditions I described earlier? Perhaps a hint of something holy? Do you see Christ coming to earth to pay a price to redeem His bride, just as that young Jewish boy had to pay a bride price to the father of the girl? Do you remember how in John 14:2–3, Jesus said He was going to "prepare a place" for us, much like that Jewish boy left the betrothal intent on building a home for his bride? And finally there is that impromptu whisking away of the virgin bride, an event that reflects a future occasion when Christ will return for His bride, the church, and we will be taken away to live with Him.

What a romantic wedding feast there will be on that day. More on that later, but for now know this: only those who believe in Him and have professed Him as Lord and Savior will be taken up to live with Him.

It is an exclusive love.

Just like marriage is meant to be.

What Is Marriage?

Marriage embraces the mystery of male and female differences and brings them together in an exclusive love commitment. *Yada* is "a sensory awareness...attained through involvement."[3] This sensory awareness, this knowing of each other, requires that the two parties be "located 'opposite'"[4] one another but so close that they are "with" or "one."[5] Can you think of anything other than a man (designed to fit into a woman) and a woman (designed to fit with one man) that could possibly be opposite and yet within? Only a consummated marriage relationship between one man and one woman can fit this description in the physical realm.

Ancient Jewish culture placed that first sexual union just before the lengthy wedding feast (but after much tradition and ceremony in the engagement period that we forgo). Our modern Christian culture honors the exclusivity of sexual union by placing it just after the tradition and ceremony, which ends with a shorter wedding feast. But in each instance, the sexual union points to the deep knowing and respect of *yada* that is found only in an exclusive love relationship.

So we find ourselves in the New Testament period of history. You and I, here, betrothed to Christ our Savior. (There's so much to learn from God's definition of the marriage union!) The New Testament continues the work of teaching us about *yada*, but by using a Greek equivalent: *ginosko*.

> Then Mary said to the angel, "How can this be, since I do not know [*ginosko*] a man?"
>
> —LUKE 1:34, NKJV

> When Joseph woke from sleep, he did as the angel of the Lord commanded him: he took his wife, but knew [*ginosko*] her not until she had given birth to a son. And he called his name Jesus.
>
> —MATTHEW 1:24–25, ESV

The world did not know [*ginosko*] Him.

—JOHN 1:10, NASB

You will know [*ginosko*] the truth.

—JOHN 8:32

I know [*ginosko*] my sheep.

—JOHN 10:14

That I may know [*ginosko*] Him.

—PHILIPPIANS 3:10, NASB

We are reminded once again of that holy representation of knowing God relationally, pictured in the intimacy and exclusivity of knowing a husband physically.

Maybe I'm making a big, fat, hairy deal out of words, but I don't think so. I'm just certain enough that God breathed each word of Scripture, to believe that He selected each word with care. So let's see what God wants us to learn at this touchpoint of redemption, when Christ comes to earth to rescue His bride.

Just as our relationship with Christ is a covenant relationship, sealed in His own precious blood, so too is marriage a covenant. A covenant is

a binding, unbreakable obligation between two parties, based on unconditional love sealed by blood and sacred oath, that creates a relationship in which each party is bound by specific undertakings on each other's behalf. The parties to the covenant place themselves under penalty of divine retribution should they later attempt to avoid those undertakings. It is a relationship that can only be broken by death.[6]

In a covenant of such permanence, one member of the agreement is a representative. The representative guarantees the covenant. In our covenant relationship with God, Jesus is our guarantor. He promises eternal life through the giving of His own life. In God's valiant attempt to rescue us from the Villain, a payment had to be made. The cost was

the gift of Motherhood

"That ain't no Etch A Sketch. This is one doodle that can't be undid, Homeskillet."

"It's probably just a food baby. Did you have a big lunch?"

"They were talking about in health class how pregnancy...often lead[s] to an infant."

Juno. In a rare moment of cinematic insight, a pregnant teenager bypasses the abortion option, and the life of the baby is uplifted as sacred. The Sunny D–drenched child is gifted to an infertile woman with a mother's heart.

Why does this movie capture our hearts? I think it has something to do with Juno's "wondering if two people can great, and only the representative could speak to the payment. I find it ironic that in John 19 when Jesus was brought to Pilate, the words Pilate used align so beautifully to this need. After Jesus was beaten and crowned with a ring of thorns, Pilate turned to the religious leaders and said, *"Ecce Homo."* In English, "Behold Man." In Latin, there was no definite article. Pilate didn't say, "Behold the man," or, "Behold a man." He said, "Behold Man." He was saying, in essence, "Here is humankind." It may be a stretch, but in some ways it was like saying, "This man is the representative. He will pay the price. Let the rest go free."

What holy passion.

What exclusive love.

stay together," and her noble act to give life. Under all our feminism-influenced values lies a craving to "stay together" and *then* to nurture. In *Juno,* we are comforted by the fact that a baby is protected and applauded as valuable.

Genesis 1:28 notes, "God blessed them and said to them, 'Be fruitful and increase in number; fill the earth and subdue it.'" It is the first command for man and woman. We are told to have babies. And I can tell you from experience that it's the most fulfilling thing a woman can ever do.

I hope you'll consider what God writes in His Word about the precious honor of being a mom, rejecting the feminist mentality that denies our hearts this amazing gift.

"The bottom line is this," writes Lauren Winner:

> God created sex for marriage, and within a Christian moral vocabulary, it is impossible to defend sex outside of marriage.[7]

In light of His purpose to portray His image (relational love) and His salvation (exclusive love), it is impossible to consider God's guidelines for sex as arbitrary. Nor can we label them as outdated or old-fashioned.

God's call for sex to be preserved for one man and one woman who have not even a hint of sexual experience anywhere else is in context with His plan to portray Himself and His love to a lost world. I believe the exclusive passion and commitment of a bride and groom is meant to be a picture of an exclusive, exciting relationship with Jesus Christ that is free from any other gods. When people witness the passion and mystery of that rarely seen couple who are still emotionally engaged with each other "after all these years," it gives credence to the possibility of something lasting and passionate. And the apostle Paul said such a relationship will be so rare in our world that it will be called a "mystery." He went on to say it will make people hungry for the mysterious, exclusive love of Christ.[8]

I've got to leave my writing cabin. In a couple of hours I'll be at Olive Garden, giggling with Cali, the blushing bride-to-be, and the rest of our crew. But I'm so honored to celebrate this covenant with her.

I just have to share a couple photos with you. Cali's fiancé, Peter,

is a graphic artist and designer. As such, he not only constructed the most romantic proposal you can imagine, he had the foresight to have it photographed. First, he walked her out beside a beautiful lake. Then he read from a journal they'd been passing back and forth for some time. (He'd write his love to her, then she'd write hers to him.) On this occasion, he'd written something he wanted to read *to* her. A long testimony of his love for her and everything he loved about her. His dreams for their future. And then a question. To read that, he got on one knee.

And just as she erupted into a joyous "Yes!"…

…God cued His creation to kiss the moment.

So here are Cali and Peter. Engaged. Eighty-one days away from their wedding feast. (But who's counting?) And we are working together to make this bride ready.

And on another level of romance, here's the church. Engaged. Not sure how many days we have until the wedding feast. But I am working to make this bride ready by keeping her pure and spotless.

Are you?

the line

the conversation between my two college-aged interns and me went something like this:

ME: What is the burning question about sex on the minds of college-aged women?

COURTNEY: "Where's the line?"

BRIANNA: Bam! That's it.

COURTNEY: The lines are wishy-washy. Everyone knows, "Don't have sex." What does *that* mean?

BRIANNA: Like with kissing. Where's the line with kissing? What kind? How much?

COURTNEY: According to everything I've heard at [Christian college], kissing is okay. Sex is not. Everything else is up to you.

BRIANNA: Like, is *fondling* okay? No one ever says.

COURTNEY: My fiancé's youth pastor told him that anything above the belt is okay.

BRIANNA: *What?* You've got to be kidding me! That is going to be in the book!

I can tell you that Courtney's fiancé's youth pastor is a *complete bonehead*! (And the names in this story have been kindly changed to protect him, though he does not deserve it.) The theology in Beyoncé's song "Single Ladies" is better than his. (But catchy as it is, it's not really a great message when you consider it carefully.) I think we all have to be careful not to listen to Christian idiots who don't take the time to examine the Scriptures for truth and often justify sin while ignoring the exclusive love of *yada*.

In this chapter I'm going to use the truth of the Bible to try to answer everything you ever wanted to know about the ever-popular question: how far is too far? Lean in for the 411 about everything one-on-one.

Let's shoot straight. There's a lot of sex going on out there. Roughly 75 percent of high school students graduate as nonvirgins.[1] If you're on a public college campus, roughly 81 percent of the students you encounter are sexually active[2] (probably not hard to believe given the Walks of Shame you witness Sunday afternoons). When I was interviewing students at Penn State, I talked to one girl who was noticeably different from the others. Her name was Shannon. She had a brightness in her eyes and a freedom in her spirit that set her apart from so many of the girls I talked to. I would even call her sassy. Shannon is a virgin, but that has been a costly decision for her.

"Other students brag during class about specific stuff they did with guys," reported Shannon. "Of course, I really don't get involved in the conversation because I don't go to the parties."

Then she raised her chin a little and held her shoulders higher as she said, "Some of my friends don't understand why I don't go to the parties, but I've never felt the desire to get into the party scene. And because of that, I feel I'm more in control of my life."

As I write this, Shannon is studying art history abroad. She's in Rome, having the time of her life. What a contrast to many young women I work with, who are so worried about a short-term relationship falling apart that they stay close to home rather than exploring and taking advantage of God's gift of singleness.

Another student I spoke with had been temporarily caught up in the party and sex scene but soon felt the shallowness of it. When she pulled out, she experienced the same kind of ridicule from her friends. This prompted her to ask me:

> Why is there tolerance for everything but sobriety and abstinence here? Aren't those healthy choices worthy of respect?

Frankly, I've wanted to ask the leadership of secular college campuses that same question on a number of occasions. But rather than encouraging self-control, they often spend time writing noncommittal, legally vetted, public nonapologies for unfortunate occurrences on

Sex on Campus

The amount of sexual activity on college campuses varies quite a bit, depending on the type of institution. Research shows that 81 percent of students at state colleges and universities are fully sexually active. On the average Catholic or private secular campus, roughly 65 percent admit to hooking up. And on an evangelical Christian campus, only 21 percent acknowledge having engaged in full sexual intercourse.[3]

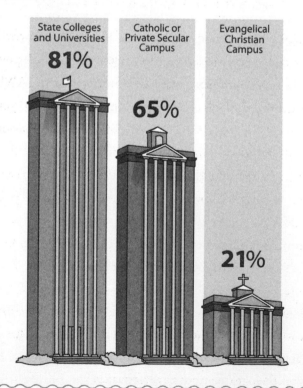

State Colleges and Universities
81%

Catholic or Private Secular Campus
65%

Evangelical Christian Campus
21%

campus related to drinking, drugs, and promiscuity. The letters, of course, have to be written with a voice of "tolerance." The local media tend to turn a blind eye to the illogical contradiction of tolerance, never taking time to build an atmosphere of approval for safer, healthier choices. And so it goes. You and I live in a world that's completely intolerant of sexual purity and self-control.

So what's okay? How far is too far? I'm going to break this down using the actual questions that the college-aged women I consulted asked me to answer in our private, no-holds-barred meetings.

"Where's the Line with Kissing?"

Good question and a good place to start. Kisses can be sweet and innocent or dangerously seductive. To understand the full power of a kiss, let's explore your body's autonomic nervous system (ANS). This is the system that controls fear (like the time you crunched your dad's car and your body went into instant hot-flash mode), Pavlovian responses (like when your mouth waters because you smell the Auntie Anne's Pretzels stand), and sexual stimulation (like that pleasant flutter in your tummy when your guy brushes his lips across your cheek and you take in his scent).

These responses are not controlled by your mind. You don't say to yourself, "Huh. I just ripped off the front fender of my car. I think I will choose to sweat now." Instead, the autonomic nervous system instantaneously reads the situation and sends signals to your other body systems, which trigger you to sweat, salivate, or swell. This is where kissing can get dangerous and why it's vital to categorize kisses— much as seismologists categorize earthquakes.

A pleasant closed-mouth kiss can create a mini–autonomic nervous system tremor. Let's say a 1 on the Richter scale. Barely perceptible. You may feel a pleasant rush of connection, but nothing gets too out of control. While I've encouraged my kids to save that first kiss as long as they can and share it with someone special (like maybe their fiancé), I'm not going to argue that you absolutely *can't* kiss. The Quick and Innocent Kiss probably won't get you into trouble.

But then there's the kind of kiss that sets off a sizable 6 on the Richter scale. You know the kind. The Make-Out Madness Kiss may or may not be survivable. I don't have to describe it, but your mouth is now a little more engaged, along with, ahem, your tasting sensations. Remember that autonomic nervous system? You just sent his into overdrive (and maybe yours too). For us women, the ANS response is a little slower, but the guy's is immediate and powerful (they say, sexually speaking, that women are like Crockpots and men are like microwaves). Very specific body responses begin to occur with this kiss, and they can create an intoxication that blinds you. Proverbs 5:18–19 says,

> Rejoice in the wife of your youth....
> May you ever be captivated by her love.

The word *captivated* would be better translated "intoxicated." That's what the ANS does. It intoxicates. You remember that great chemical dopamine, which God created to cause a wife to be addicted to her husband? Well, it's potent, like liquor. And it actually does intoxicate you. Once you get it flowing, it is really difficult to even remember why you'd want to stop.

Finally, there's the Perfect-Ten Horizontal Hookup Kiss. Once you're lying down, those tremors are so powerful that they're bound to knock over some of the values you've built up. Stay vertical.

Basically, keep the seismic world quiet by putting boundaries on kissing until you *are* the wife of his youth.

Fondling?

Another good question, since we're looking at Proverbs 5:18–19. Did you notice the ellipses in the earlier quote? I left out some pretty key words in the verse. It actually looks a little more like this:

> Rejoice in the wife of your youth.
> A loving doe, a graceful deer—
> may her breasts satisfy you always,
> may you ever be captivated by her love.

That last sentence, if you look at the Hebrew, would be better translated, "May you ever be *intoxicated* by her *sex* or *sensuality*." (Push pause: it is remarkable to me that God had Solomon, in his generously endowed wisdom, write in this verse about a body system that science had yet to discover. Okay, push play.)

You were created with a great power to intoxicate with your sexual beauty. But check it out: this seduction is happening between a wife and her husband. And how many wives? It says, "Rejoice in *the* wife." One wife. Your breasts were made for how many men? One! How convenient that God made this nice and clear.

Yada calls you to be known by one man in an exclusive love relationship. This implies that you are unknown to others. That includes your breasts! It's right there in black and white. (So much for low-cut shirts, tight camis, and letting your lacy bra peep out the top of your shirt line!) God wants you to be exclusive not just in what you let a guy touch with his hands, but in what he caresses with his eyes as well!

Let me explain a little bit more about how that chemical factory inside your head works, the one we talked about several chapters ago. Introducing the female sexual superglue: oxytocin. (Guys have one too. It's called vasopressin.) Oxytocin is released when a woman climaxes sexually. It washes over her brain in generous amounts, creating a bond that makes her desire contact again and again with the same man. It's God's design for protecting the marriage relationship. Dr. Joe McIlhaney, founder of the Medical Institute for Sexual Health, observes,

> The desire to connect is not *just* an emotional feeling. Bonding is real and almost like the adhesive effect of glue—a powerful connection that cannot be undone without great emotional pain.[4]

Oxytocin isn't created *only* during intercourse and orgasm. A woman's body also creates it with meaningful skin-to-skin contact.[5] It's a chemical your body enjoys in many beautiful ways. Your guy holds your hand? Oxytocin! You enjoy a Quick and Innocent Kiss? Oxytocin! He brushes your hair with his hand? Oxytocin! Each touch creates emotional glue. (God will even use this chemical to bond you to your babies. As you breast-feed them and hold them? Oxytocin!)

here's the rub

My husband, Bob, says, "Ninety-six percent of massages lead to sex." Let me think... Yep! Pretty much that's it. Skim back through the chapter for details on ANS and sexual superglue to understand why. You might want to give your guy (and your guy friends) a break and just save the rubdown for after the wedding ring.

Note: no scientific trials or data whatsoever were used to support this conclusion!

Read this: any guy who likes what's above the belt better "put a ring on it"! That's not to suggest that an engagement ring is enough. I'm talking about the wedding ring. On the day you say "I do," you'll get your license to touch. Until then, stick to some tender handholding.

Is Oral Sex Really Sex?

Once, when I was speaking at a Christian event on a secular college campus, a couple approached me. He was a football player—all but worshiped in the college town. Proud as could be, he stood beside his girlfriend to tell me that they were using his "celebrity" status to encourage purity on the sex-stained campus.

"Whenever we get the chance, we share *our* philosophy." He beamed—with a touch too much pride, I might add.

Noticing a distinct look of shame on her face, I felt the need to clarify. "What is *your* philosophy?"

"We just stick to oral sex," he said.

She burst into tears.

I spent some time talking with this couple and discovered that she knew they had taken things too far; she just didn't want to risk losing the relationship. (Oh, how *many* girls I talk to who fall for that lie.) The truth was, he really loved her and was trying to protect and respect her, but he'd never been given any good teaching on just how to do that. He could sense that the oral sex was actually hurting their

where's Your line?

I've found that thinking it through ahead of time helps you call a halt to production when the chemical factory kicks into gear. Want to protect your purity? Pick a place to draw the line below, and make a mental plan to adhere to that standard!

10. Sexual Intercourse

9. Oral Sex

8. Mutual Masturbation

7. Breast Fondling

6. The Horizontal Make-Out

5. The Vertical Make-Out

4. An Open-Mouthed Kiss

3. A Soft Kiss

2. Holding Hands

1. A Steady Gaze

relationship, but he didn't know why! He was utterly ruined that he'd caused her to hurt so badly. Together they made a commitment to hold to a higher standard, and I made sure they had a mentor to help them move forward with some accountability. She didn't lose him by speaking her mind. In fact, the honesty and commitment to purity made their relationship better.

But this couple is not alone in their confusion about where to draw the line. Roughly 50 percent of college students have had oral sex in the past thirty days.[6] I'm saddened by how common this has become and mortified that so many justify it by claiming it's not really sex.

Oral sex exposes a woman to the same emotional connection and intimacy that vaginal intercourse does, as well as the same sexually transmitted diseases. In recent years, HPV (the primary cause of cervical cancer) has also been linked to throat cancer.

And last I checked, they don't call it *oral friendship*.

It is sex.

And it's way past the line for any single girl who looks forward to one day enjoying *yada* with her husband.

We could probably go on like this for a while. Christian women who want to live in purity desire concrete answers. I get that. But I think we might be asking the wrong questions altogether. I think the real issue isn't "How far is too far?" What is really being asked in that question is this: "Just how much can I get away with?"

Instead, maybe we should be asking how we can carefully avoid anything that would cause that autonomic nervous system to kick into seismic, cataclysmic intoxication. And God gives us a verse that draws the line rather clearly:

> But among you there must not be even a hint of sexual immorality, or of any kind of impurity, or of greed, because these are improper for God's holy people.
>
> —EPHESIANS 5:3

Looks to me like the virginity line is not our standard for purity. (I know a lot of virgins who are anything but pure. And I know a lot of nonvirgins who are living beautiful lives of purity after learning from their mistakes.) We aren't supposed to be finding out just how close we can get to that virgin line without sinning. Instead, we are to be pursuing a life that is free from any hint of sexual sin.

So let's commit together to asking this question on a regular basis: *Lord Jesus, how have I hinted at sexual sin?*

~~~~~~~~~~~~~~~~~~~~~~~~~~~~~~~~~~~ 13

starting over

my husband may have thought he'd married the virgin of all virgins. Little did he know, my virtuous conduct in our relationship was fueled by the sad experience of my sexual sin. Our dating relationship, chronicled in *And the Bride Wore White,* was a truly respectful experience. Though there was sexual tension, our mutual commitment to purity kept us exploring each other's hearts rather than being distracted by our bodies. The beauty of our love magnified my ugly secret.

I tried to tell him when we looked at engagement rings together.

I tried to tell him after he proposed.

I tried to tell him when we were planning the wedding.

I tried to tell him when we got back from the honeymoon.

The thought of actually verbalizing my secret shoved me into such emotional isolation that I slept in the extra bedroom as many nights as not in the first year of our marriage. He couldn't figure me out.

I thought maybe my secret had doomed me to live in a marriage blocked from true intimacy. I believed that if I told him, he would reject me, though nothing in his behavior suggested that conclusion. My emotions locked me in an irrational prison.

Then one day, at the age of twenty-six, five years into our marriage, I was driving down the highway, listening to the familiar voice of Dr. James Dobson. My six-month-old baby girl, Lexi, was in the backseat of my brand-new white minivan. I heard two sentences that day:

DR. DOBSON: What is the number one question on a teen girl's mind when she's talking to her mom about sex?

INTERVIEWEE: The number one question on her mind is, "Mom, did you wait?"

I pulled to the side of the road and allowed ten years of grief and isolation to engulf me. The healing that I hadn't been willing to pursue for myself I finally would seek for my beloved daughter. Even before I knew her, I had written about her. My college journal—written about seven years before she was conceived—was full of musings from my heart for her, like this one:

It's so easy to fall into bad situations if you don't build up a very straightforward defense. Believe me! I know! I was just very naive and didn't have knowledge of what was going on before it happened. I hope and pray that I'll be able to know when to guide my daughter in building up defenses so she will have a little better time of it than I for waiting. I've wasted precious years of growth with the Lord. Now, it's like starting over! That's the hard way to go. I know there is no way I can decide how things will go for my daughter, but I'm praying God will give me wisdom to be her friend and guide.

So deep was the pain of my sexual sin that my prayer was for her to never know it. I had never considered that she'd ask about my past.

I knew it was time to tell Bob. I put the kids to bed, and we settled into the bedroom. I told him that I had to confess something to him.

It took me three emotionally gut-wrenching hours to bring forth a one-sentence confession. I kept turning the light off, hoping he wouldn't "see" me. He kept turning it on and holding me. When I finally mumbled an awkward sentence of truth, daring to believe that God's forgiveness was as big as He said it was, I was infused with an inexplicable sense of newness and hope.

I'd confessed my sins to God on an almost daily basis for ten years, and I was forgiven. I'd just never felt it before. Now, in my husband's arms, I *felt* it.

Perhaps that is why we are told to "confess your sins to each other...so that you may be healed" (James 5:16). As the body of Christ, we are the arms of Jesus, convincing the guilt-ridden wandering soul that it has been found by Mercy. I know that's how it worked for me, and I've seen it work that way for hundreds of other young women as I plead with them to take the first and most profound step of healing: tell someone!

I'd like to break down that simple advice into a step-by-step plan for you. Through twelve years of helping women walk into wholeness through sexual healing, I have found these to be necessary steps toward freedom from the past and victory over future temptation.

Tell an Older Godly Woman
Whom You Can Trust

The first confession is the hardest. But, according to James 5:16, it is critical to the healing process. I encourage you, whether or not you are in a dating relationship, to prayerfully consider that your first confession should be face to face with an older, wiser woman—not a guy. Don't be concerned with what you will say; just do it. It doesn't have to sound just right, and whatever you plan will probably not be what you say in the emotion of the moment.

Don't procrastinate.

Just do it.

While my first choice would be your mom, I realize that this might be too big a step for you or that your mom might not be able to handle it or that she might not be geographically available. (And I'd like you to do this within the next twenty-four hours. God is speaking to you about it now, so now is the time to pursue it.) Prayerfully consider whether it can be your mom. My own mother was such a tremendous source of healing and prayer for me when I confessed to her. I believe her intercession is one reason that I was able to move on to use my story for God's glory, rather than to continue to bury it as an unusable part of my life.

As you select the right woman, ask God to guide you to someone who is (a) older, (b) walking in strong relationship with Christ, and (c) transparent about her own weaknesses and sins. If you look for these three things, you'll often find that her response will be comforting and helpful.

Schedule a Prayer Time to Verbalize Forgiveness and Break Soul Ties

Your initial confession will probably lead to an extended conversation and perhaps some follow-up meetings to set new goals and establish accountability for existing or future relationships. (If it doesn't, let your older godly friend read this chapter so that it will.) After this occurs, it is time to take your healing to a deeper level in order for you to be prepared for marriage one day. This can and should occur within a few weeks of confession to an older godly woman, regardless of your current marriage plans or lack thereof. Why wait for healing?

Sexual activity creates a soul tie between you and the person you have sex with. When this occurs within the confines of marriage, it is a tremendous glue for the relationship. But sexual activity outside of marriage causes the soul (emotional center) to become confused. I've already explained how the brain experiences physical manifestations of our sexual choices (see pages 41–42). But let me explain it in spiritual terms. First Corinthians 6:13–17, NKJV, says,

> Now the body is not for sexual immorality but for the Lord,
> and the Lord for the body. And God both raised up the Lord
> and will also raise us up by His power. Do you not know that
> your bodies are members of Christ? Shall I then take the
> members of Christ and make them members of a harlot?
> Certainly not! Or do you not know that he who is joined to

a harlot is one body with her? For "the two," He says, "shall become one flesh." But he who is joined to the Lord is one spirit with Him.

The Greek word translated "unites" in this verse is *kallao*. It means "to glue together, to make cohere."[1] According to God's Word, anytime we have sex with someone, we are "gluing" or tying ourselves to that person emotionally. Since the soul is the center of our emotion, these are called soul ties. When these soul ties are established outside of a marriage relationship, they can wreak havoc on any future or existing marriage—havoc we can't even begin to comprehend.

A sin-induced sexual soul tie must be renounced through prayer in order to clear the way for wholeness within your marriage or future marriage. I have experienced this personally, since I did not discover my soul tie with my teen sexual partner until I was well into my thirties. The prayer that released me from this tie dramatically changed the health of my marriage with Bob.

So, your process of healing must include a specific prayer time to verbalize forgiveness toward your sexual partner(s) and to break soul ties. I generally recommend that you have *at least* two other women present for this prayer time. Jesus said that when two or three are gathered together to pray, He will be there with them.[2] (Jesus likes community!) While you can do this with just one woman, experience has taught me that it's best to have one woman directly leading you in prayer and another who has both of your backs in prayer.

Ask your older godly mentor to read the sidebar on "How to

Facilitate Sexual Healing Prayer" on page 127–130. Schedule this time together, and then begin to fast and pray for God to prepare your heart. Don't let anything get in the way of this crucial step.

Prepare Your Heart to Confess to Your Future Husband

(This might be something you won't need to do until later, so you can simply put this book aside and come back to it when you need it. I'll still be here waiting for you!)

If we are called to be intimately one within the marriage relationship, there's little room for secrets. I can't imagine living within a marriage that lacks the intimacy of transparent confession. Okay, I can actually. I did it for five years. As difficult as confessing was and is, if we practice it on an ongoing basis, our marriage is much healthier and intimate when we know each other unmasked.

However, don't go confessing to every guy you meet and begin to date or court. Wait until you are certain that the relationship is headed toward marriage. Then set a time and place to talk in private, letting him know that you have some serious things to share with him so he is in the right state of mind. In confessing to him, follow these guidelines:

1. Ask Your Older Godly Friend to Pray for You

This can be a difficult conversation, and it's good to have someone covering you in prayer and who will be prepared to talk with you afterward.

2. Confess Categorically and Truthfully

I told my husband, "I gave away the gift that God meant for me to give to you on our wedding night." And then I cried. He understood clearly that I was not a virgin. Since then, I have shared with him a little bit more but not much.

3. Do Not Confess Specific Details of Who, What, and Where

I have never—not in one relationship—found this to be helpful. Most counselors agree that specific details only torture the imagination and give root for unforgiveness. Save those details for the counseling room or to share with your mentor.

4. Be Patient with Your Boyfriend, Fiancé, or Husband (If You Happen to Be Reading This After Your Wedding Night)

He may need time to examine his own heart and respond in a godly manner. I know one woman whose husband went outside and mowed the grass. Didn't say a word. Just mowed the grass. It was an agonizing few hours as she waited prayerfully, but he came inside and was able to extend forgiveness after he processed things.

Prepare to Pass On the Healing As You Confess to Others

Second Corinthians 1:3–4 reads, "Praise be to the God and Father of our Lord Jesus Christ, the Father of compassion and the God of all comfort, who comforts us in all our troubles, so that we can comfort those in any trouble with the comfort we ourselves have received from God."

Bottom line: God doesn't heal you just to make you picture perfect. One of His purposes in giving you comfort is so that you can comfort others. The church is full of Pharisees. We don't need more of them. Rise up to be a humble example of God's mercy and grace as you share your story in appropriate places and with others who need the healing you are experiencing and living in.

Pass it on!

how to facilitate sexual healing prayer

The Scriptures teach that we do not wrestle with flesh and blood. Our battle is with spiritual, unseen forces of darkness. Perhaps the site of the most intense battle is the marriage bed, since this is a picture of Christ and the church. With this in mind, I urge you not to go into this time of healing prayer without preparing thoroughly through fasting and prayer. While I do not understand the full realm of what is done during such a prayer time, I know it is effective and I know we are always breaking some unholy bond in the person we are praying over.

To set up the prayer time, please meet with the forgiven friend—the person seeking freedom from soul ties—and verify that she is walking in a true relationship with Jesus Christ as her Lord and Savior. Confirm that she is not currently in a sexual relationship with the person you are

(continued on next page)

extending forgiveness to and seeking freedom from. Then ask her to prepare her heart with prayer and fasting as you do likewise.

Please do not go into this prayer time without preparing your own heart. Also, do not go into it alone. Make sure you have a minimum of one other trustworthy woman who can assist you in hearing from the Lord and praying for our dear sister who needs full freedom.

Once you and your prayer team have prepared your heart through prayer and fasting, there are five critical things that need to occur during the actual prayer session, which should take about one hour.

1. Ask our forgiven friend to prayerfully confess and verbalize forgiveness to her sexual partner(s). After opening in prayer that humbly acknowledges Jesus Christ as her Savior and Healer, ask her to confess her sin out loud and to specifically forgive each person she has interacted with sexually. Allow her to be specific if necessary about the sexual acts that occurred, but don't require it of her. I have found that some women need for me to know the specifics in order to believe me when I assure them of God's forgiveness. Others find a discussion of the details to be too shameful, and it closes down their spirit to the healing. During this time, you simply listen and coach her if she gets stuck. You may need to specifically ask her to say, "Lord, I choose to forgive [name] and I release him/her for [specific sin]." It is important to *choose* forgiveness, though she might not feel it. That's okay. Emotions often follow forgiveness rather than preceding it.

2. Pray in authority and ask Christ to break off any existing and unholy soul ties between our forgiven friend and her sexual partners. Pray as God leads you, using the name(s) that our forgiven friend just spoke, and ask God specifically to break off any bondage or ties to each one. You can say something like, "Lord Jesus, we ask You to break off the soul tie that exists between [forgiven friend] and [name of sexual partner] in Your precious name and by the power of the Holy Spirit."

3. Ask God to reveal any lies about herself or her relationship with God that may have taken root in her heart. Often we internalize terrible lies. Lies commonly believed by young women I have prayed with include, "I can never serve God now," or, "My body is bad," or, "I'm a whore,"[3] or, "Men are bad." You can learn more about how to get to the root of a lie in the book I cowrote with Nancy Leigh DeMoss titled *Lies Young Women Believe,* but in general you have to rely on reading your friend's cues and asking the Holy Spirit to reveal the lie to you and to her. As He does, find specific Bible verses to pray over her that state truth. For example, if she believes the lie that her body is bad, turn to Psalm 139 and read it over her.

(continued on next page)

4. Verbalize God's forgiveness to your forgiven friend. Take a lot of time, and specifically tell her how proud you are of her and why. Read scriptures that you've selected from your preparation and prayer time to encourage her.

5. Send her home with a list of Scripture verses about forgiveness to study and memorize. God's Word is the only true power I have ever discovered that effectively reprograms a broken emotional system. Often the wounded person believes lies about herself and needs God's truth to retrain her heart and mind. As you pray, speak aloud specific verses that come to mind and assign one member of the prayer team to write these down. If you haven't found any during the prayer time, close by prayerfully asking God what our forgiven friend needs to take home with her. Ask her to put these verses where she can read them several times a day and program her heart and mind to believe them.

finding *yada*

talk about a tug of war!

Sometimes getting between a girl and her parents can pull you to pieces. A few years ago, I met a young woman—a really amazing, intelligent, driven, purposeful, beautiful college girl who was dating someone not like her. Her parents, who were as beautiful as she was and acted like they were still twenty—in a good way—and were actively involved in youth ministry were *freaked out*! In their opinion, the guy was not following after God and had no ambition. He'd dropped out of college and was just hanging out most of the time, while occasionally working a minimum-wage job. Oh, and during his short stint at college, he'd cheated on their daughter. They asked me to meet with her.

I got her side of the story. From her perspective, he was a new believer and she'd given him freedom to date other people when he went away to college. And even though she'd previously broken up with him because he was pressuring her sexually, now she was convinced he was really trying hard to walk with God and needed some grace. She felt like he'd changed his ways, and she was fairly certain he was "the one." As for her parents, "They're being legalistic. Doesn't a guy who has repented deserve a little forgiveness?" she asked.

I certainly felt like I needed the wisdom of Solomon. I asked her if I could take some time to pray about it and answer her question when we met again later that night. I spent my afternoon in the hotel room asking God for some direction, and the truth He led me to that day has become a wellspring for a hundred girls asking the question, *How do I know if he's the one?*

First, let me say that only you and God can fully determine if he's "the one." But God has put certain things into your life to help you with the decision. (After all, way too many of us girls have taken the plunge into marital bliss based solely on chemicals, only to regret the decision.)

God has given us older, wiser people like our parents, pastors, and mentors to encourage and caution us. You should always give them your ear and check their input against one another to make sure they are hearing from God and not their own hearts.

He's also given us friends to pull us out of the inclusive date trap and keep us grounded.

And He's given us His Word.

What?

You missed the passage on "how to find a mate in three easy steps"? Me too. Until just this past year. But it's right there in black and white:

> Husbands, love your wives, just as Christ also loved the church and gave Himself up for her, so that He might sanctify her, having cleansed her by the washing of water with the word, that He might present to Himself the church in all her glory, having no spot or wrinkle or any such thing; but that she would be holy and blameless. So husbands ought also to love their own wives as their own bodies. He who loves his own wife loves himself; for no one ever hated his own flesh, but nourishes and cherishes it, just as Christ also does the church, because we are members of His body.
>
> —EPHESIANS 5:25–30, NASB

I know, I know. It sounds like a passage instructing husbands on how to treat their wives, right? Well, let's just dissect it a little bit, and you'll see that it's also a plethora of knowledge about how to know if he's the one. Let me show you.

"Gave Himself Up for Her"

The guy you want to marry is one who *will* give himself up for you and who *is* giving himself up for you. What does that look like when you're nineteen and at a singles party? It looks like the guy who lets all the girls go first before he grabs his turn in the pizza line. It looks like the guy who carries your luggage on the missions trip. It looks like the guy who opens your car door and pulls out your chair when he takes you on a date.

You see, to give himself up for you, he has to be completely in tune with your every move and need. He has to be denying himself in small ways so that he's capable of giving himself up in bigger ways when you are married one day. Do you know many guys like that? I think they used to call them gentlemen!

The guy who is "the one" will give himself up for you. I'm reminded of Luke Myers, who noticed my new college-aged intern, Molly Brown, a few years ago. Molly had never had a boyfriend. Ever. She was a beautiful, soft-spoken, giggling Southern girl who firmly believed in the romance of asking God for just one man! Not many. So she wasn't that impressed when Luke started to show an interest in her. She was only a sophomore and thought it was too soon to meet "the one."

So Luke gave himself up for her. He backed off, but just a bit. He gave her the space she felt she needed. Oh, he hung out with her and they developed a friendship in group settings. (They made Meyer Dairy a frequent stop with many friends and ate their fair share of grasshopper sundaes at The Corner Room.) And then Molly's internship ended and she went home, taking Luke's heart. But he gladly gave it to her.

And kept waiting.

All the while, he offered what Molly calls "a patient pursuit." His was a heart of gentle romance bridled by much prayer.

A few months after she moved away, Molly realized that she missed her patient and selfless friend Luke. And their love life began, culminating in a great wedding celebration in December 2008. I recently vacationed with the two newlyweds, and I can tell you that restraining his passion did not ultimately deny Luke what he wanted. In fact, his bride is quite awestruck with him now…to the point of making even a lover of romance like myself quite nauseated if I stay in their presence too long!

It is the rare relationship that is entrusted to God and born out of self-restraint, the giving up of emotions, drives, and passions. But those are the ones where the passions seem to run most deeply when the time is ripe.

"Washing of Water with the Word"

The apostle Paul's language here is pure, 100 percent Middle Eastern, circa first century AD. You see, in those days Jewish brides were prepared for marriage with a ceremonial bath. The spiritual parallel is that Christ has washed His bride, the church, through His death. But His once-for-all sacrifice means all the old ways of "making things clean" are gone. So Paul introduces a new way to cleanse a bride. Now she will be cleansed ceremonially by one thing and one thing alone. Not water, but the Word…and not before marriage, but as a continual action after marriage. That means your man will pour Scripture over your life!

What's that look like for you today? It means you'll get more than text messages that read, "<3 You're still the one. 4EAE. <3." Instead you might get one that reads, "Ecclesiastes 4:12!" (Way more romantic!) Rather than a private chat on Facebook that's all about the drama of life, you'll find yourselves chatting about the promises of God for your life. It means he'll share Scripture with you to encourage you to exchange a bad or less-than-ideal behavior for God's best.

This is never forced or contrived, or it doesn't count. This guy is so into God's Word that it's natural for him to share something from it when you're together. This is not to be confused with the guy who is so full of himself that he thinks he is God's personal voice of truth for you! Dump that one for a more humble model...one that demonstrates an ability to be convicted by God's Word and comes with tender encouragement for you.

The guy who is "the one" will wash you with the Word...and do so with humility!

"Having No Spot or Wrinkle"

Jesus Christ's goal was to make us acceptable to be in the presence of God the Father. So He purified us by dying to Himself. It is the awesome and weighty responsibility of a husband to mirror this kind of love by presenting his earthly bride to God as pure and spot-free.

This isn't rocket science: the guy who is "the one" will not ask you for what you should not give. Instead, he will crucify his flesh to protect your purity.

I remember a moment when Bob did this for me. We had been engaged for several weeks and had not seen each other since the day after he proposed. He finally got some time off from his new job and drove late into the night to visit me. I was waiting in my little apartment in Cedarville, Ohio. Upon his arrival, we melted into each other's arms, and within moments he was lying on top of me on the sofa. (Richter scale alert!) My jean-clad butt had barely touched the cushion when he jumped up, pulling me with him. Then he pushed me away and ran out of the apartment. I stood there for a moment, feeling rather rejected, then followed him outside. He promptly

Worth the Investment

Every single year, I give the "Finding Your Million Dollar Mate" message to the seniors at Grace Prep, the high school my husband founded. The students have practically memorized the message, based on a book of the same title by Randy Pope. The concept centers on the simple idea that there are three parts to each person:

1. BODY
2. PERSONALITY
3. SPIRIT

You can't really trust the first two parts of a person not to change. Go ahead; pick a guy because he's got a great set of glutes. Their value will decrease with time. His personality? They say that changes every ten years. The only sure investment is his spirit. If his spirit is connected to the Spirit of God, it is the only part of him guaranteed to increase in quality and value.

Looking for a Million Dollar Mate? Invest in one with the right spirit!

announced, "You're too *much* for me. We're going to Deb Haffey's."
Dr. Haffey was our college professor, and she babysat us all week-
end. That's what it took to crucify his flesh, so that's what my fiancé
did!

The guy who is "the one" will protect your purity, not try to take
it from you.

"Nourishes and Cherishes"

In some translations, this phrase is translated as "feeds and cares for."
Christ feeds us and nurtures us, and so must a husband take care of his
wife. Just as we become a member of Christ's body, so a husband and
wife become one. And one practical aspect of this relationship is his
role in feeding and caring for you. That means he will be responsible
with his schoolwork and his finances. It means he'll be motivated and
able to provide for you. He'll be working hard as a student of excel-
lence or have a job where he works equally hard (maybe both). He's
motivated to do this, in part, by the dream of taking care of you.

I had the coolest conversation with my twenty-year-old son, Rob,
the other day. A junior at Penn State Schreyer Honors College, he is
taking classes in engineering that go way over my head! He's surrounded by friends who are "in relationships." I wondered if this both-
ered him or if he was looking extra hard for "her." So, being the mom
who always gives her kids space (read with sarcasm), I asked. His answer was so amazing. It went something like this: "I'm studying right
now. That takes a lot of time, and I wouldn't be able to devote much
time to a relationship. I'm doing this now, so I can meet her later."

(I'll give you a moment to recover. And, no, you cannot have his e-mail address.)

The guy who is "the one" will be motivated to feed and care for you, to nourish and cherish you by taking care of your physical needs. This hard-working guy is worthy of the respect *yada* demands, not a guy with no work ethic.

I think it's important to note that this is written by a woman who happily supplies the lion's share of her family income. When publishing success came my way, my husband did not shrink from it or become dependent on my hard work. Instead, he participates in it, *giving himself up for me* as he manages my contracts and marketing. He also has a second job where he manages a vision that God has given to him for a new model in education, which is being realized at Grace Prep. I'm not so old-fashioned that I believe a man who cares for you needs to be the sole provider. I do believe he should take a lead in ensuring the provision for a home. And my man is strong enough to do that with a strong woman under his wings!

I took this passage of Scripture to the girl who was dating the guy her parents thought was a loser. She'd asked, "Doesn't he deserve forgiveness?"

I told her yes. "He does deserve forgiveness. He does. From you and from your parents."

Then I said, "The question is not whether you should forgive him. The question is this: is he 'the one' according to God's definition?"

I think a lot of the young women I counsel about relationships are asking the wrong questions when they look for Mr. Right. They ask things like,

"Doesn't he deserve forgiveness?"

"How much should it matter that I am physically attracted to him?"

"Isn't there an emotional feeling you get that he's the one right away, and why didn't I get that?"

I could go on. The questions are as interesting and varied as the women who bring them, but they are the wrong questions. The right one to ask when you are seeking *yada* is this:

"Does he meet God's standard of a godly husband?"

Ask yourself that the next time you feel love in the air.

faithful love

she was a girl with a reputation.

A prostitute? That's what people said.

A promiscuous young woman? Without doubt.

Clearly she was a high-risk marriage option. But he loved her. And he felt that God wanted him to marry her. So instead of another one-night stand followed by a Walk of Shame, she got a marriage proposal.

A girl with her reputation would be a fool to pass that up. She was working the oldest profession in the world. He was a well-respected community leader. So the wedding invitations were printed, the bridesmaids and groomsmen gathered, and the music swelled. The wedding feast celebrated new love.

The celebration was short-lived.

Apparently the only big change for her was the label on her behavior, not the behavior itself. The whore became an adulterer. Baby number one looked a little like her husband and an awful lot like the guy she'd been rumored to be with. Baby number two? Didn't look like her husband at all. Baby number three? Had they even had sex in the past year? After all, she hadn't slept at home in a long time.

But he still loved her.

So goes the story of the prophet Hosea and his beloved but wandering wife, Gomer.

The day comes when she's not even living with Hosea. Either she's sold herself into sex slavery, or she's the mistress of another man. Whatever the situation, it'll take money to get her back this time. God actually tells Hosea to pony up the cash: "Go, show your love to your wife again, though she is loved by another and is an adulteress. Love her as the LORD loves the Israelites" (Hosea 3:1).

Is this love story about Hosea and Gomer?

Or about Yahweh and Israel?

Both.

It is about both. Just as your earthly love story is a picture of God's love for His people.

I've learned something as I've been writing this book: the deep romance of *yada* is not attained through the beauty and innocence of the lovers. That's baby love. That's an unmessy beginning. An erotic yearning that wants something not yet fully known.

Yada requires something more. It is realized in imperfections and craggy disfigurement, hidden beyond the unblemished innocence of not knowing. *Yada knows.* It knows the unwelcome, unsightly secrets—secrets that could rightfully prompt rejection. But *yada* overrides the logical desire to dismantle the wounded relationship. *Yada* reaches into the grace-filled depths of unconditional staying power and finds the strength to breathe life into love one more time.

Yada is a faithful love.

A staying love.

Perhaps more than any of the other characteristics of *yada*, *faithful* love resonates deeply with my heart because it calls me to hope. Not just in Bob and Dannah. But in Jesus and Dannah. In Jesus and the oh-so-wounded church. Ezekiel wrote about this faithful love when he recorded these words:

> Yet I will remember the covenant I made with you in the days of your youth, and I will establish an ever-lasting covenant with you.... So I will establish my covenant with you, and you will know [*yada*] that I am the LORD.
>
> —EZEKIEL 16:60, 62

God's *relational* and *exclusive* love illuminates a picture of hope in His covenant, which promises *faithful* love. This covenant, sealed in the blood of our Savior, will be brought to fullness when we move beyond the engagement (or betrothal) of the church to finally be married. That will happen on the great day of "the marriage supper of the Lamb" (Revelation 19:9, NASB). It's then that we'll experience the fullness of God's faithful love, as described in the book of Revelation.

The author wastes no time in conjuring up the imagery of romance between our Savior and His bride, the church. The very name of the book invites us into the mystery of the love and suggests a consummation. Dr. Scott Hahn, in *The Lamb's Supper*, explains,

> The term *apokalypsis*, usually translated as "revelation,"
> literally means "unveiling." In John's time, Jews commonly
> used *apokalypsis* to describe part of their week-long wedding
> festivities. The *apokalypsis* was the lifting of the veil of the
> virgin bride, which took place immediately before the marriage was consummated in sexual union.
>
> And that's what John was getting at. So close is the unity
> of heaven and earth that it is like the fruitful and ecstatic union
> of a husband and wife in love.[1]

My friend, this is why we were created: to experience relational, exclusive, faithful love with God. We were created to be in rich, intimate communion with God and those who love Him. What a party it will be! Everyone celebrating the most romantic story in history. The rescue of the bride who was, after all, always intended and spoken for.

And I believe it will be a celebration of the Savior's personal love for each and every one of us, as well as a communal love. There, in the richness of community, your Savior will come to you. He'll get off His white horse and take your hand. Gazing directly into your eyes as if no one else is nearby, He'll lead you to a table set for two. Seating you there, He'll speak the name only He has for you and only you will hear. It is your love name. Private. Secret. Just for you. He's had it written on a white stone for some time, pining for you.[2] I guess He could have written it on the bark of some tree, but then again, it might not have lasted had it not been written in stone.

> He chose us in Him before the foundation of the world,
> that we should be holy and without blame before Him
> in love.
>
> —EPHESIANS 1:4, NKJV

He's been waiting since before the creation of earth for this moment.

Waiting for you.

This is what you were created for.

Every other act of communion is just a mere foreshadowing of this. True love between one man and one woman is just pointing toward this, like prophecy.

The Undying Faithfulness of *Yada*

To know. To be known. To be deeply respected.

I've known this kind of love in my marriage. Like CPR for a lifeless body, forgiveness fills the emptiness of my spirit and rescues me from among the walking dead. Without the awareness of another spirit's (Bob's) knowing my deepest darknesses—along with my passionate desires—I'm not truly certain of my value to "be" at all. This is the heart of *yada*. To be known—just as we are—and still be pursued.

I knew that love this week. I was a sinful woman. It is always my tongue that trips me up. I say things I shouldn't. I drop little bombs here and there that leave marks, and this week I dropped the Hiroshima of atomic bombs. I used my words to wound Bob with his past.

romantic Overture

The covenants of God are always declared complete in the celebration of a meal. The meal demonstrated that the two representatives of the covenant—who drank from the same cup and ate from the same bread—were one (*echad*). That's why you and I enjoy a covenant meal in the act of communion.

"He was known [*ginosko*] to them in the breaking of bread" (Luke 24:35, NKJV). In taking the bread and the cup, we are giving physical expression to our relational, exclusive, faithful love with Jesus Christ. It is in that deep act that we express to Him our knowing and respect. And that rich sharing will culminate at the Marriage Supper of the Lamb. You see, the act of Holy Communion is just a romantic overture to the banquet of consummation that we are invited to attend.

It created a two-day standoff.

In the end, we drove home from our small group and sat in the driveway for a long talk in my black Envoy. There were a lot of tears. A lot of accusations. A lot of apologies.

And sometime during that gut-wrenching conversation, my heart became fully alive. Somewhere in the depths of working it through, I knew I was faithfully loved. Still. Even though.

Once again, *yada* triumphed, and we walked past the past.

Past my PMS and his depression.

Past my sexual brokenness and his fight to be mentally pure before God.

Past my uncontrolled tongue and his lack of being present.

That's *yada*.

How do I know that this brokenness, followed by hard staying power, is actually a part of *yada*?

Hesed.

Hesed is one of the words frequently used parallel to *yada* in the Old Testament. When you find a deep knowing (*yada*), you will often find *hesed*, which is to say you find deep friendship, unfailing love, loyalty, devotion, steadfastness, mercy. *Hesed* is faithful love.

Malcolm Smith says that *hesed* "probably ranks among the most important words of the covenant." He notes that "it describes that the relationship is being worked out; it is the covenant in action. So when Scripture is speaking of *hesed*, it is often in the context of His *doing* and *showing* and *keeping* the covenant when every word that has been sworn to is put to the test."[3]

Hesed is what makes *yada* a "staying love."

> Therefore know [*yada*] that the LORD your God, He is God, the faithful God who keeps covenant and mercy [*hesed*] for a thousand generations with those who love Him and keep His commandments.
>
> —DEUTERONOMY 7:9, NKJV

David called on God's "staying love" when he was in deep darkness. He'd committed adultery with Bathsheba, then killed her husband in battle to cover up his sin. Upon discovery by the prophet, the king knew there was no forgiveness under the Law of Moses. He should have been stoned to death. But David cried out,

> Have mercy [*hesed*] on me, O God, according to your unfailing love; according to your great compassion.... For I know [*yada*] my transgressions, and my sin is always before me."
>
> —PSALM 51:1, 3

Apparently God's love trumped the law even back in the day. David lived and went on to be "a man after [God's] own heart" (Acts 13:22). Despite all his ugly secrets, God's "staying love" closed the gap between them.

That is the kind of love He wants you to know in marriage.

It's the kind of love I've known, in spite of my brokenness. In spite of Bob's.

My love life with Bob can be seen in these other love stories. We are...

Gomer and Hosea.

Israel and Yahweh.

Dannah and Jesus.

We wander sometimes. Like Gomer strayed from Hosea. Like Israel strayed from Yahweh. Like Dannah strays from Jesus.

As I finish up the edits on this book, I miss my Savior. It's been a season of such busyness that my heart is not nestled into His. While I usually sit at His feet for an hour a day, these past few months I've wandered into a lazy time of walking my dog while I listen to worship music. It started out as a nice change, but I was duped. When I began writing this book, I was full of the Spirit of God by feasting on the Word, prayer, and worship. As I end, I'm thirsty and discouraged. I wish I wasn't, and it feels ugly, and writing this book feels hypocritical.

try it before you buy it?

"You gotta try it before you buy it." That's what one FOX News commentator actually said when covering the love story of Claudaniel Fabien, thirty, and Melody LaLuz, twenty-eight—abstinence educators in Chicago's public school system who did not kiss until their wedding day.

"Garbage," was the news commentator's assessment of their decision.

"I give 'em six months," said the other male commentator. (Not kidding. I saw it on YouTube.)

But the female commentator said, "I love this idea.... Women love this! They just talked for three years."

She saw what I see. Your relationship can really be tested as you get to know each other (not your bodies) and find out if you actually like each other and not the sex. I'm pretty sure the honeymoon for Claudaniel and Melody went just fine.

If you "try it before you buy it," what's left to discover and be thrilled about?

But that *is* the beauty of faithful love. Because despite the flaws and offenses, we still *are*. I'm undeniably tethered to my Savior, and my grief is evidence of that. After countless spiritual seasons of victory and then some of being ever so broken in the battle, our love still *is*. That's the staying power of *yada*.

Faithful Beginnings

A dating or courting relationship will tell you how well equipped a guy is to exercise the staying power of faithful love, both with you and with God. I'm reminded of a young woman I counseled who was utterly heartbroken over her sexual past. In a moment of intoxicating insanity, she'd given her virginity away. Now she was engaged to a different guy and had just told him about her past. His response: "I forgive you, but I need to think about this. Can I have some time to decide if I still want to marry you?"

Of course, he could and should have time, but he was taking weeks. Weeks after her confession, he still hadn't called. Hadn't written. Nothing. Nada. Zip. Mutual friends told the wounded young woman that he was worried about his image, and his family was concerned that this would "hold him back in ministry"!

I'm angry just writing those words. I could just spit fire at a guy like that in hopes that it would purify the conceit and pride right out of him! Jesus was certainly not into image management. And a guy you commit to love exclusively can't be either.

"Dump him," I counseled the girl. "He doesn't have staying power. He lacks faithful love. Do you really want to spend your entire life trying to measure up to his unholy, pharisaical standard of perfection?"

She did dump him. (And then her mom and some other godly women used the Sexual Healing Prayer, found in chapter 13, to bind up her broken heart.) Today, she's a young bride, happily married to a man whose response to her past was filled with the promise that he had faithful, staying love!

Oh, please know that I have rejoiced at many weddings where two virgins are joined together. I pray for more weddings like that, but the sad fact is that many of us are broken, and all of us are imperfect. And we need some faithful, staying love to even get us started!

Such was the love found by one of my favorite girls. I met Lauren when she was fifteen and a new Christian. Her boyfriend had led her to Christ. Then he tried to lead her to bed. She said no, and it took a few boxes of Kleenex for her and me to get her heart straight when they broke up.

Then she went to college and met Kevin, who told her, "I'm going to wait to kiss my bride for the first time on our wedding day."

Lauren laughed. "Good luck finding that girl!"

Kevin went on to explain. He'd fallen many times. Knew his body was sometimes stronger than his spirit. He wanted to be known as a guy who protected girls, especially the girl he most loved. That meant he had to take even kissing off the table. It was too much for him. Created an override in his normally self-controlled character. So, no kissing until "I do."

The girl who would marry Kevin would know his past. His weakness. His hurt. And she'd share in it through self-restraint.

Of course, that girl was my girl: Lauren!

I was present when Lauren and Kevin kissed for the first time. Right there in front of a few hundred of us. What power was in that kiss. It was ecstasy and forgiveness. Knowing and discovering. It was sexy and holy.

It was a faithful beginning.

the yearning

have I mentioned that sex is fun?

I meant to.

How did we get so far along without the fun stuff? I guess I'll have to write about that in a book for you to use *after* your wedding day! But let's at least peek under the covers before we close the pages of this one.

One of the most popular books about sexual pleasure is the *Kama Sutra*. Written by Vatsyayana, a Hindu philosopher, it claims to be the first book written on the art of lovemaking. (At a glance, it seems to be purely about physical pleasure, but it is rooted in Eastern mysticism and many of the sexual positions are modified Hindu worship positions.) In her applause for this book, Bobbi Dempsey, author of a tragically confusing modern book on sexual pleasure, says that "Christian and Jewish texts and teachings contain no mention of…sex. In fact, these two religions make little or no connection between sex and worship at all."[1]

Mind if I blow this out of the water?

In truth, of all the world religions, Christianity alone boasts the most radical of holy books. Perhaps you've heard of it? It's called the Song of Solomon, or Song of Songs. This celebration of unashamed physical pleasure stands out uniquely among religious books. Written in approximately 970 BC, it beats the *Kama Sutra* by 1,320 years. How's that for a thrashing?

The Jewish faith—and Christianity, which adopted its divinely inspired literature—wholeheartedly embraces physical pleasure in this book (and others within the Bible). For example, the Song opens with these words:

> Let him kiss me with the kisses of his mouth—
> for your love [or lover] is more delightful than wine.
> Pleasing is the fragrance of your perfumes;
> your name is like perfume poured out.
> No wonder the maidens love you!
> Take me away with you—let us hurry!
> Let the king bring me into his chambers.
>
> —SONG OF SOLOMON 1:2–4

This poetic and graphic overture unashamedly expresses the passionate desire to experience physical pleasure. Wrought with references to touch, teasing, verbal tantalization, and shameless tasting, the first chapter of the book invites, "If you do not know [*yada*], most beautiful of women, follow the tracks…" (verse 8). Clearly, *yada* includes great physical pleasure.

Sex Is Fun

Sex was created, in part, for pleasure.

Okay, just for the sake of giving you something to consider, I asked a few young women who grew up under my purity ministry and then married as virgins to discreetly share some of their thoughts on the gift God has given to them.

> When I respond to or initiate sex with him, it makes him feel secure.
>
> ———
>
> We did it four times in one day on our honeymoon! Just one day! [Just so ya know, that's not very typical!]
>
> ———
>
> During our intimate experiences, we are at our most vulnerable state.
>
> ———
>
> We are having more fun than I ever thought possible figuring it all out. Sometimes we just fall down naked in laughter as we enjoy the gift. It's amazing!
>
> ———
>
> Wow!

I don't want to go all formal on you, but you should know that research suggests that these young wives might not have enjoyed this depth of pleasure had they tasted too much too soon. A study conducted by the University of Chicago, and considered to be one of the most statistically accurate studies on sexuality available today, determined that the most orgasmic women in the United States are middle-aged, married, conservative Protestant women, with 32 percent claiming that they climax with orgasm every time they have sex. Mainline Protestants and Catholics were just behind them at 27 and 26 percent respectively, but those with no religious affiliation claimed to have orgasms only 22 percent of the time. Furthermore, those having the most sex were not singles, but women in monogamous marriages—and they liked it more than the singles.[2]

Girl, if you choose to do this God's way, you've got some mind-blowing pleasure coming your way!

Let me go back to Song of Solomon for just a moment, because I recently learned something that radically changed my view of this book. You see, I'd always assumed that everyone considered the book allegorical. That is, the lovers are representations of God and the church. Turns out, not everyone believes that. Some really heavy-weight Bible scholars believe that the book is a literal celebration of the deepest encounter that a man and woman can share together.[3] Author and church planter C. J. Mahaney writes,

> Spiritualizing the Song of Solomon just doesn't make sense. What's worse, it denies to us the powerful impact God intends for it to have on our marriages.[4]

Some scholars suggest that perhaps Solomon is not the author, or that he wrote it but not as a description of his own love life. Consider the fact that the poem is about one man's love for one woman. It can hardly be about Solomon since he had as many as three hundred wives and up to seven hundred concubines (mistresses for the express purpose of his sexual pleasure).

What makes more sense to me is what Pastor James MacDonald suggested on his radio program *Walk in the Word:* that it was written by Solomon as he observed a love so pure and tender that he pined for it.[5]

In other words, Solomon penned a poem to honor a relational, exclusive, faithful love that he *witnessed* but never knew. Solomon's life was characterized by going along with his culture's sexual norms. He had many wives because that's what political players did

thirty-day media fast

I believe that the greatest hindrances to understanding sexuality and knowing God are the deceptive messages we absorb each day through music lyrics, television shows, movies, and even comments on our social media forums— messages that contradict God's truth.

Want to really get it? Try a thirty-day media fast. Just get unplugged from the world for thirty days. Take all the time you would normally give to listening to mainstream music, watching TV or movies, and socializing on Facebook, and instead invest it in your relationship with God. (Ironically, when you plug back in, let me know how it goes by commenting on my Facebook page!)

in 970 BC. And yet his poem cries out to celebrate a one-man/one-woman, loyal, playful sexual relationship in a society where the number of wives indicated the level of a man's power. The poem tragically expresses a craving for *yada* by a man who had experienced only its counterfeit, *shakab*.

Spiritual Confusion

I mentioned earlier in the book that the word *yada*, as used in Scripture, emphasizes the role that the heart plays in perception, in intimately knowing the other party. By contrast, perception can be impeded by "confusion" of the heart or spirit.[6]

I believe that we live in a sexually confused day and age, and many hearts and spirits cannot perceive or know God. Like so many in Solomon's day, we've missed the beauty of *yada*, not only in our human love relationships but also in our interactions with God. So many long for something deeper and richer, but they don't know if it's even possible.

It doesn't have to be this way.

I'm pleading with you to reject our culture's norms. It may be the norm to have friends with benefits, send sext messages, or have multiple sexual partners, but those hollow counterfeits will only bring destruction of your heart and body. Instead, step up! Be bold enough to experience the temporary pain of self-restraint in the pursuit of *yada*. Do it not just for the benefits you'll experience in your own life, but ultimately so that the world can see the God who loves them.

As Peter Jones, a professor at Westminster Seminary, says, "If Christians do not find the courage to address the biblical teaching on sex, they will wake up one day to find themselves and the gospel completely marginalized."[7] You see, it is within *yada* love that the world sees a picture of God's relational, exclusive, and faithful love. The world cannot see Him or His love if we do not live according to the sexual theology that God has written for us. In light of this, His guidelines about our sexual behavior aren't as arbitrary as some might have you believe.

All of which brings me to this: You will never have enough head knowledge or emotional passion to successfully govern your sex life according to God's very difficult standard of purity. To pursue and experience *yada*, you have only one hope: to know God. As Pastor John Piper so eloquently put it in his book *Sex and the Supremacy of Christ*,

> 1) *Sexuality is designed by Christ as a way to know God more fully;* and 2) *knowing Christ more fully in all his infinite supremacy is designed as a way of guarding and guiding our sexuality.* All sexual corruption serves to conceal the true knowledge of Christ, and the true knowledge of Christ serves to prevent sexual corruption.[8]

I guess that's what I've been trying to say in a few dozen pages. Pastor Piper says it in two sentences!

Do you desire to experience *yada*—a sexuality that's fulfilling and real and everything God designed it to be? You must press into knowing God. His heart contains the only path to true sexual intimacy with an earthly love.

A few years ago I found a great Christian quote on a T-shirt that sums it all up. (I haven't been able to find the original source for this quote.) Here's the bottom line:

> A girl's heart should be so lost in God that a guy has to seek Him to find her.

That's it.

Know Him.

And you'll have what it takes to know him one day.

Yada.

Know Him.

Make Him known.

I've made my case. I've answered your burning questions, and now I have one for you.

You know the one Truth that explains what you're waiting for.

What will you do about it?

DISCUSSION QUESTIONS

If you really want to get the most out of this book, read it with a group of friends, and discuss the concepts. This will give you a chance to internalize your personal beliefs as they are challenged and built upon in this book. The discussion guide has been created to cover all sixteen chapters over the course of eight weeks. Read just two chapters a week; then meet to talk through your thoughts.

Chapters 1 and 2

1. On which side of the sexual debate do you find yourself: sexual freedom or chastity belts? Why?

2. In what ways was it helpful to get into Dannah's heart concerning her past? What part(s) of her story in chapter 2 do you identify with?

3. Read 2 Corinthians 1:3–4. Dannah found comfort when she reached out for healing from her past. She believes that she can look at it as an opportunity to comfort others with the comfort she has been given from God. In what areas of your life has God comforted you, enabling you to pass that comfort on?

Chapters 3 and 4

1. Have you ever found the arguments for sexual purity to be trite or boring? Where are they most effective? What elements are missing? What would engage you—or what arguments

might you use to convince a friend that sexual purity is a choice worth making?

2. Describe the word *yada*. How does this word impact your preconceived ideas about sex?

3. Read Psalm 139:1–4, 13–16, 23 again. God has "before love" for you. What does this mean to you? Do you believe it? Why or why not?

Chapters 5 and 6

1. Describe the word *shakab*. In what specific ways have you seen culture advocate this counterfeit by depersonalizing sex?

2. Dannah writes about the heart being the organ of perception when it comes to *yada*. Do you think women still want to be romanced? What would change in their behavior or perspectives if they better understood how their brains and bodies are designed to respond to sexual activity? You might take some time to research the verses in Dannah's endnote to better explore this. Check out Deuteronomy 8:5; 29:3; Joshua 23:14; 1 Kings 2:44; Isaiah 51:7; Jeremiah 24:7.

3. Read Titus 2:11–15. According to this verse, what enables us to say no to worldly passions? How can you experience God's grace in practical ways so that you can say no to worldly passions?

Chapters 7 and 8

1. Relational love, as seen in marriage, helps us to understand the relational character of God. When have you witnessed relational love in marriages around you? Describe what you have observed where relational love is missing.

2. Dannah focuses a lot on the unique qualities of women that tend to intrigue men. What are some of the really cool points of diversity that make a guy mysterious to you?

3. What are some sexual lies or labels you have lived under? Can you think of a specific Bible verse to contradict your lie? You'll note that there's no verse in this week's discussion. That's so you can find one that is personal to you and make that your meditation today as you close.

Chapters 9 and 10

1. What's the Hebrew definition for sin, or *chatta,* that Dannah introduces in chapter 9? How does it help us to define sexual sin?

2. What is the primary issue with both masturbation and porn that misses the mark of God's ideal?

3. Read Job 31:1. What did Job do to avoid lustful thoughts? How can you make a modern-day covenant with your eyes?

Chapters 11 and 12

1. Exclusive love helps us to understand the intimacy God wants to have with each of us. Talk about how a newly married couple has an exciting, romantic, exclusive love. What qualities do you think characterize that love? What connections do you see between their love and your relationship with God?

2. How does viewing sex as a picture of God's love help you to understand God's rules about sex? What aspect of those boundaries is still hard for you to understand or conform to?

3. Where do you draw the line for physical contact with a guy? Why?

4. Read Ephesians 5:3. What is God's standard for purity in your life? How can you pursue this?

Chapters 13 and 14

1. How does Dannah's story of healing make you feel? Do you need some healing?
2. Read James 5:16. How do we experience healing? Who have you confessed your sin to? How is that helping you to heal and to be more accountable in future choices?
3. Which of the four qualities of a husband, as described in Ephesians 5, means the most to you? Do you believe a guy like this exists for you? Why or why not?

Chapters 15 and 16

1. Faithful, staying love gives us an understanding of God's faithfulness to us. What Hebrew word did Dannah say is often used along with *yada* to communicate faithfulness? How does this concept impact your view of romantic love?
2. Song of Solomon is unabashedly explicit about the pleasures of intimacy. How can the idea of sexual pleasure be a motivator to exercise self-control?
3. Read Song of Solomon 7:10. Soak in this verse. Then take some time in your group to pray that God would turn the desire of one man toward you, in His right timing.

ACKNOWLEDGMENTS

I have wanted to write this book for almost a decade. After I discovered the rich trail of truth that the Bible modestly veils within a single Hebrew word and the plethora of answers we find when we dare to follow it, the message of this book became my *life* message. If only I could get the world to see what I was seeing!

But…it wasn't time yet. I didn't even try to find a publishing partner because I felt the Spirit of God holding me back. "You have more to discover. Follow the trail a bit longer." I had so much more to learn—and still do. This truth is that rich! But one day I suddenly felt God's release: "Now, go! Go! Go!"

So I stopped along the way of my wanderings to put my vision into a book proposal. Within just a few days, I gave it to my dear friend, agent, and Starbucks addict Mike Keil of The Resource Agency. He successfully got a pretty good handful of acquiring editors and publishers to consider it, but only one saw in this precious trail the invitation of a journey for every believer. Her name was Laura Barker. And like a seasoned tracker, she caught the rich scent of the trail along with me. So much of this message is hers now. She saw things I did not as we walked together. She directed my passion into something that would cause others to want to follow. No one else has leaned into the effort along with me as she has. I'm so grateful to call her a friend and can't wait to get back to Colorado Springs to share adoption stories in a daylong editing marathon that begins with a much-too-early break-fast and ends with a late-night dinner!

Laura started and steered the vision at WaterBrook Multnomah, but my gratitude for this skilled team does not end with her. What an honor to have publisher Ken Peterson take a personal interest in the project, actually reading and speaking into the finished form. Vice president Carie Freimuth, who has worked on some of my favorite projects in the publishing world, honored me by being involved in making this one a success. Allison O'Hara steered the ever-vigilant marketing team. Laura Wright took care of details as the production editor. And thanks to Leslie Seetin for making my book cover one that I can love. Hope you do too!

A few others caught up with Laura and me on the journey. A special thanks to Craig Weidman (Eastern PA District of the Christian and Missionary Alliance) and Professor Daniel Estes (Cedarville University), who provided insightful theological reviews. Andy Mylin provided some funky graphics. And though they do not realize it, two men have provided significant stops in the journey that fueled my passion. Malcolm Smith, *The Lost Secret of the New Covenant* is the only published book in which I have seen an author address this precious and significant word. You inspired me when I thought perhaps I didn't know what I was seeing. Thank you for seeing it too! Peter Jones, author of *The God of Sex,* thanks for hosting the think tank event "The Sexual Body: The Epicenter of the Worldview Battle," which helped me to further form my thinking.

Where would I be without my dad and mom, Dan and Kay Barker, who continue to love and support my work? It cannot go without mention that I wrote this and most of my books at their lovely mountain home, where I can hear only the sounds of birds and the voice of God.

Finally, thanks to the one who continues to walk the trail with me after two decades of hills, valleys, and mountaintops. Bob Gresh had "before love" for me, experienced the newness of passionate early love, and continues to love me through my faults, fears, and failures. Along the way, we found the Enemy of humankind hidden in the dark corners near the trail, seeking to ravage our love and tear away any hint of the mystery that could incite curiosity for a Greater Love than humans can ever offer. We've taken a few hits, but we are now more in love and full of discovery and mystery than at any point in our marriage. As we prayed on our wedding day, may you see the love of Christ for the church in our love for each other.

NOTES

Chapter 1

1. Gracie Murano, "7 Wedding Proposals Gone Bad," Oddee, www.oddee.com/item_96647.aspx.

Chapter 3

1. It would be overstating the case to say that each biblical occurrence of *yada* speaks of God-honoring sexuality. It is used in other instances, as I'll share later in the book. But I believe that the word *yada* points to the nuance of deep experiential and emotional knowledge, and I'll prove that as we move through this book.

Chapter 4

1. "Dating Customs Around the World," Fact Monster, www .factmonster.com/ipka/A0767654.html.
2. See Psalm 9:10; Jeremiah 5:1; Numbers 22:19—but not until you get to the end of this chapter!
3. Psalm 139:7.
4. Malcolm Smith, *The Lost Secret of the New Covenant* (Tulsa, OK: Harrison House, 2002), 61–62.
5. John Piper and Justin Taylor, *Sex and the Supremacy of Christ* (Wheaton, IL: Crossway, 2005), 26.

Chapter 5

1. The word *shakab* can be used in positive or neutral senses as well
   when it is used outside of the context of sexuality. However,
   when the term is used for sexual activity, it usually (and perhaps
   always) refers to perverse activity, in contrast to the positive sense
   of *yada*.

2. *Key Word Study Bible* (Chattanooga, TN: AMG Publishers,
   1996), Hebrew word number 8886.

3. Donna Freitas, *Sex and the Soul: Juggling Sexuality, Spirituality,
   Romance, and Religion on America's College Campuses* (New York:
   Oxford University Press, 2008), 152.

4. Valerie Frankel, "Click Here for a Good Time," *Self* (November
   2009), 130.

5. Waffle-Woman-X3, a reader who commented on an article
   entitled "50 Edward Cullen Characteristics That Every Guy
   Should Have," Fanpop, www.fanpop.com/spots/twilight-series/
   articles/3218/title/50-edward-cullen-characteristics-every-guy
   -should.

6. Huei-Hsia Wu, "Gender, Romance Novels and Plastic Sexuality
   in the United States: A Focus on Female College Students," *Journal of International Women's Studies* 8, no.1 (November 1, 2006),
   125–34.

7. Frankel, *Self,* 130.

Chapter 6

1. Ernst Jenni and Claus Westermann, *Theological Lexicon of the
   Old Testament,* Volume II (Peabody, MA: Hendrickson, 1997),

512. Spoiler alert: don't look up these verses until you've finished this book or you'll lose the impact of what's to come as we unfold the great power of this word. However, the following passages speak to the heart's involvement in the true perception that occurs in *yada:* Deuteronomy 8:5; 29:3 (eyes and access were not enough to *yada*); Joshua 23:14; 1 Kings 2:44; Isaiah 51:7; Jeremiah 24:7.

2. As quoted in Chrissy Iley, "Kate Hudson on Life and Love," *Sunday Times,* December 21, 2008. http://entertainment .timesonline.co.uk/tol/arts_and_entertainment/film/ article5358178.ece.

3. I heard Pastor Ted Hamilton say this during a keynote message at the 2009 TruthXChange think tank "The Sexual Body: The Epicenter of The Worldview Battle." His message on Creation Sexuality is, to this day, the most profound message on sexuality I have ever heard.

4. George Vaillant, "Why We Love," *Discover Presents the Brain,* Fall 2009, 27. An article reprinted from George Vaillant, *Spiritual Evolution: A Scientific Defense of Faith* (New York: Broadway, 2008), 94.

5. Claus Westermann, *Genesis 1–11* (Minneapolis: Augsburg Fortress, 1994), 288–89.

6. Kirk Johnson, PhD, Lauren Noyes, and Robert Rector, "Sexually Active Teenagers Are More Likely to Be Depressed and to Attempt Suicide," June 3, 2003, on the Web site of The Heritage Foundation, www.heritage.org/Research/ Reports/2003/06/Sexually-Active-Teenagers-Are-More

-Likely-to-Be-Depressed. I often come across studies that support the idea that the suicide and depression rate is higher among sexually active teens than among those who remain abstinent.

7. Eileen L. Zurbriggen, PhD, et al., "Report of the APA Task Force on the Sexualization of Girls" (American Psychological Association, Washington, D.C., 2007), www.apa.org/pi/women/programs/girls/report-full.pdf.

8. Lauren Winner, *Real Sex* (Grand Rapids: Brazos, 2005), 88.

Chapter 7

1. These hilarious quotes came from "Kids Say The Darndest Things," *Tribe,* http://entertainmentquotes.tribe.net/thread/0e8b2545-6bd4-4730-8969-d801ece0f3b2.

2. Rob Lowe, "What I Know Now...That I Wish I'd Known Then," *Glamour British* 103 (October 2009), 156.

3. Bobbi Dempsey, *The Everything Tantric Sex Book* (Avon, MA: Adams Media, 2007), 4.

4. Peter Jones, *The God of Sex* (Colorado Springs, CO: David C. Cook, 2006), 76.

5. There is a component of emotional behavior that seems to be nurtured by environment. A little girl's brain has more capacity for verbal skills and emotions, whereas boys tend to be more hyperactive and physical; yet the brain is very elastic and can be modified by environment. For a great theological view of this, see Judith K. Balswick and Jack O. Balswick, *Authentic Human Sexuality: An Integrated Christian Approach* (Downers Grove, IL: InterVarsity, 2000).

6. As quoted in "Dear John," *Glamour British* 103 (October 2009), 225.

7. Dominic West, as quoted in "How to Give a Dream Interview," *Glamour British* 103 (October 2009), 168.

8. Mark Bieganski, "We Just Want to Have a Baby Now," The Oprah Blog, *Chicago Sun-Times,* April 3, 2008, http://blogs .suntimes.com/oprah/2008/04/we_just_want_to_have_the _baby.html (accessed June 29, 2010).

9. Philip Yancey, *Rumors of Another World: What on Earth Are We Missing?* (Grand Rapids: Zondervan, 2003), 88.

Chapter 8

1. Beth Moore, *Praying God's Word* (Nashville: Broadman and Holman, 2000), 235.

2. Nancy Leigh DeMoss and Dannah Gresh, *Lies Young Women Believe: And the Truth That Sets Them Free* (Chicago: Moody, 2008), 32.

Chapter 9

1. Valerie Frankel, "Self-Pleasuring While Looking at Online Porn: Who's Doing It?" *Self* (November 2009), 131.

2. Valerie Frankel, "Why We Surf for Sex: Real Women Fess Up," *Self* (November 2009), 130.

3. I reached out to some friends for prayer and accountability. I soon began to experience freedom.

4. Some erroneously refer to the story in Genesis 38:8–10 of Onan, the son of Judah, who was having sex with his dead brother's wife (yeah, kinda gross). He let his semen fall on

the ground, and this displeased God. It displeased God because it was selfish and against the command for Onan to create offspring for his brother as an act of kindness to provide for the widowed woman. But there is no direct teaching in the Bible concerning masturbation.

5. Steve Gerali, *The Struggle* (Colorado Springs, CO: NavPress, 2003), 50.

6. Retrieved from oChristian.com, http://christian-quotes .ochristian.com/christian-quotes_ochristian.cgi?find=Christian -quotes-by-Watchman+Nee-on-Self-control. Watchman Nee, *The Spiritual Man,* vol. 3 (Anaheim, CA: Living Stream, 1992), 655.

7. Judith K. Balswick and Jack O. Balswick, *Authentic Human Sexuality: An Integrated Christian Approach* (Downers Grove, IL: InterVarsity Press, 1999), 41.

8. Lauren Winner, *Real Sex* (Grand Rapids: Brazos, 2005), 55.

Chapter 10

1. Timothy C. Morgan, "Porn's Stranglehold," *Christianity Today,* March 7, 2008, www.christianitytoday.com/ct/2008/march/ 20.7.html.

2. Katleyn Beaty, "Not Just a Guy Issue: Crystal Renaud Helps Women Addicted to Pornography." *Christianity Today,* April 21, 2010, www.christianitytoday.com/ct/2010/april/27.80.html (accessed October 13, 2010).

3. Bob Gresh, *Who Moved the Goalpost?* (Chicago: Moody, 2001), 53.

4. "Obsessed and Consumed: Emerging from the Prison of Pornography," *The Promise Keeper* newsletter (July/August 1998), 1, quoted in Bob Gresh, *Who Moved the Goalpost?* (Chicago: Moody, 2001), 50.

5. Naomi Wolf, "The Porn Myth," *New York,* October 20, 2003, http://nymag.com/nymetro/news/trends/n_9437.

Chapter 11

1. Age of brides taken from various sources, including "Wedding Trends in Canada," *Wedding Bells,* www.weddingbells.ca/results; staff writer, "Statistics on Weddings in the United States," *Sound Vision,* www.soundvision.com/info/weddings/statistics.asp; Sheila Sullivan, "Bridal News Network Trend Report," *Bridal News Network,* www.bridalnewsnetwork.com/BNN%20 Trend%20Report.pdf; "What Is the Average Age at Marriage Worldwide?" *Wise Geek,* www.wisegeek.com/what-is-the -average-age-at-marriage-worldwide.htm; and Rob Davis, "The Summer Wedding Survey," *UKBride,* www.ukbride .co.uk/pages/home/rotating-home-articles/the-big-bride -survey-2010.

2. As quoted in Natasha Courtenay-Smith, "Let's Hear It for Being Single," *Glamour* (October 2009), 82.

3. Ernst Jenni and Claus Westermann, *Theological Lexicon of the Old Testament, Volume II* (Peabody, MA: Hendrickson, 1997), 511.

4. Jenni and Westermann, *Theological Lexicon of the Old Testament,* 511. The text cites as examples Psalm 51:5; 69:20.

5. Jenni and Westermann, *Theological Lexicon of the Old Testament,* 511. The text cites as examples Isaiah 59:12; Job 15:9; Psalm 50:11.

6. Malcolm Smith, *The Lost Secret of the New Covenant* (Tulsa, OK: Harrison House, 2002), 12–13.

7. Lauren Winner, *Real Sex* (Grand Rapids: Brazos, 2005), 29.

8. Ephesians 5:3, 31–32.

Chapter 12

1. Centers for Disease Control and Prevention. Youth Risk Behavior Surveillance: United States, 2005. Surveillance Summaries, 2006. MMWR 2006; 55 (No. ss-5).

2. Donna Freitas, *Sex and the Soul: Juggling Sexuality, Spirituality, Romance, and Religion on America's College Campuses* (New York: Oxford University Press, 2008), 162.

3. Freitas, *Sex and the Soul,* 163.

4. Naomi I. Eisenberger and Matthew D. Lieberman, "Why Rejection Hurts: A Common Neural Alarm System for Physical and Social Pain," *Trends in Cognitive Sciences* 8, no. 7 (July 2004), summarized in Joe S. McIlhaney and Fred McKissic Bush, MD, *Hooked: New Science on How Casual Sex Is Affecting Our Children* (Chicago: Northfield, 2008), 37.

5. This chemical was also designed by God to bond us to our children. When a woman goes into labor, she begins to produce copious amounts of oxytocin. And each time she experiences nipple stimulation during breastfeeding, it is sent out across her brain, creating a beautiful mother-child

bond that, as with the marital relationship, should never be broken.

6. McIlhaney and Bush, *Hooked,* 75.

Chapter 13

1. Spiros Zodhiates, ed., *The Complete Word Study Dictionary: New Testament* (Iowa Falls: IA, World Bible Publishers, 1992), #2853, 875, quoted in Beth Moore, *Praying God's Word* (Nashville: Broadman and Holman, 2000), 232.

2. Matthew 18:19–20.

3. I find it ironic that through the counseling and prayer process, the word *whore* is commonly used by a girl to describe herself. If she were to use a more common, contemporary word, I might not find it odd. But this is an older, vulgar term that isn't coming out of her daily living experience; it's coming out of the dark recesses of her thoughts. For this reason I am led to believe that it's a demonically driven thought. I believe the thought goes deeper than just a bad feeling. Her use of that word is a sign that the Enemy of her soul has been messing with her mind. I do everything I can to use God's written Truth to rip that word out of both her vocabulary and her heart.

Chapter 15

1. Scott Hahn, *The Lamb's Supper: The Mass As Heaven on Earth* (New York: Doubleday, 1999), 125.

2. Revelation 2:17.

3. Malcolm Smith, *The Lost Secret of the New Covenant* (Tulsa, OK: Harrison House, 2002), 41–42.

Chapter 16

1. Bobbi Dempsey, *The Everything Tantric Sex Book* (Avon, MA: Adams Media, 2007), 157.

2. Robert T. Michael et al., *Sex in America: A Definitive Survey* (Boston: Warner Books, 1994), 129.

3. Scholars who hold this view include James MacDonald, John Piper, Warren Wiersbe, Victor Shepherd, Adam Clarke, Thomas Constable, Jeff Miller, Lloyd Carr, and Sidlow Baxter.

4. C. J. Mahaney, "Sex, Romance, and the Glory of God: What Every Christian Husband Needs to Know," in John Piper and Justin Taylor, eds., *Sex and the Supremacy of Christ* (Wheaton, IL: Crossway, 2005), 154. (The Mahaney material can also be found in expanded form in his book of the same title.)

5. James MacDonald, "Romantic Love Is Exclusive," April 13–14, 2010, and "Romantic Love Is Expressed," April 15–16, 2010, *Walk in the Word,* podcast audio, www.walkintheword.com/podcast.xml.

6. See Deuteronomy 29:4; Isaiah 29:9–12; Jeremiah 5:3–5; and Psalm 95:8–10.

7. Peter Jones, *The God of Sex* (Colorado Springs, CO: David C. Cook, 2006), 9.

8. John Piper and Justin Taylor, eds., *Sex and the Supremacy of Christ,* 35.

MEET DANNAH GRESH

The world has been lying to us. It's time for some good truthful girl talk about guys, beauty and modesty. Pure Freedom is a live event based on the book *What Are You Waiting For?* Join Dannah live to follow the trail of one provocative, ancient word through the Bible to discover just what God has to say about purity, true beauty and modesty!

A LIVE EVENT!
www.purefreedom.org

People in the Bible didn't wait to have sex until after the wedding...

why should we?

Dannah answers your toughest questions at dannahgresh.com

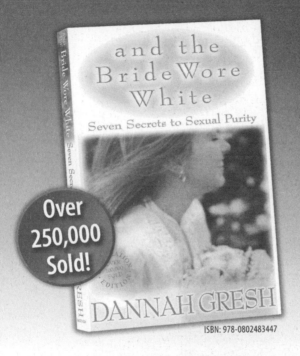